THE BEST OF

'Breakfast with Dave,'
Vol. I

A Taste of Jokes, Stories and Menus

BY JAMES V. COLUBIALE

LifeRich Publishing is a registered trademark of The Reader's Digest Association, Inc.

LifeRich Publishing books may be ordered through booksellers or by contacting:

LifeRich Publishing
1663 Liberty Drive
Bloomington, IN 47403
www.liferichpublishing.com
1 (888) 238-8637

ISBN: 978-1-4897-2298-0 (sc)
ISBN: 978-1-4897-2297-3 (e)

Print information available on the last page.

LifeRich Publishing rev. date: 06/16/2019

ACKNOWLEDGEMENTS:

Anthony J. Colubiale: Chief Administrator for http://breakfastwithdave.wordpress.com/

Paul J. Mathis: Blog Editor-in-Chief.

IN MEMORIUM: Doug "The Calculator" Letterman

And the following faithful participants who have helped keep the spirit of Breakfast with Dave alive over the last ten years:

Frank Ackley	Carmen Alessi	Lorraine Bianco
Bernie Bishoff	Ina Brown	Sandra Brown
Joan Burkhart	Bill Carr	Thomas Costello
Susan Crossan	Rick Ferrante	Lou Ann Gable
Janice Gallagher	Bill Garrison	Jerry Gius
Linda Gruchowski	Ed Jurewicz	Lisa Jurewicz
Bert Kern	Stan Kotzen	John Kovacs
Nan LaCorte	Lynn Massimiano	Micky Matracchio
Wayne Mazurek	Ray McAlarnen	Mary Lou McCall
Bill Noe	George Pagliaro	Jack Pftizenmayer
John Quinn	Pat Quinn	Jim Ridgeway
Steve Riley	Ed Sherretta	Gail Tweed
Becky Vance-Wilson	Bonnie Walker	Henry Wiegel
Jackie McKnew	Betty Ann Sherretta	Merc Bauman
John Wilsey	Lorinda Hanna	Dr. Richard Strauss
Jim O'Neil	And, of course, Dave Smith.	

"It's not a small world; it's a big Cape May."

--Larry Brown

DEDICATION:

This book is dedicated to the loving memory of "Sir" Paul J. Mathis, a friend, colleague, and confidant and one of the founding fathers of 'Breakfast with Dave' whose spirit continues to pervade each and every Thursday morning's gathering of the Tribes.

INTRODUCTION…

Over the last ten years of my retirement, I have grown to appreciate two quotes. The first is by a famous One-Hundred acre wood denizen named Winnie, the Pooh, and it goes like this: "They say nothing is impossible, but I do nothing all day!"

The other simply states: "When I wake up, I have nothing to do (all day)! By the time I go to bed, I'm only halfway done." However, even these two quotes cannot express just how great retirement actually is. I highly recommend it; everyone should experience it.

Some people do retirement better than others, but even those people have days that regretfully slip much too fast through their hands. As a result, in retirement, friendships could fade away rather quickly. So, ten years ago I decided to email my fellow retiree Jim and suggested we meet for breakfast and catch up. As Jim was about to respond to my request, he received a call from our mutual friend and newly retiree, Paul. When Jim told Paul about the idea, Paul said, "Breakfast with Dave? I'm in!" And so 'Breakfast with Dave' was born. We decided to meet every Thursday at 9 AM at a different breakfast establishment each week. Soon, fellow retiree Ed Jurewicz became the fourth regular member of the Thursday morning breakfast club.

After a few years of weekly gatherings, Jim started a "Breakfast with Dave" blog, which, at one point, had over 6,000 hits. Several of our colleague retirees began reading the blog and then joined in on the Thursday fun themselves. Our numbers only grew from there. Now, our group must call ahead to ensure that the diner or café can seat, as a group, the 8 to 12 people that could possibly show up. We once had 18 retired colleagues gathered to break bread together!

Along the way, we have also lost two very special people: Paul Mathis and Doug Letterman. They are remembered and missed every Thursday morning.

Finally, I have discovered that when a person is retired, the days of the week lose their "feel." Monday's are no longer dreaded. Wednesday's hump day may take on a totally different meaning, and we still have Friday on our minds. However, Thursday will always be about "Breakfast with Dave," and it shall be a blessed day!

David Smith

FOREWORD…

"Why would anyone want to read THE BEST OF Breakfast with Dave, Vol. I?"

Part of the answer to this question lays in precisely understanding what 'Breakfast with Dave' is. In Broadway Musical terms, 'Breakfast with Dave,' is "the oldest established permanent floating" breakfast in South Jersey. Every Thursday morning at 9 AM for the past ten years a group of anywhere from 8 to 12 retired Lower Cape May Regional High School teachers and staff commune together over eggs and toast with a sprinkling of some good jokes and entertaining anecdotes, as well as a little side of *Seinfeld* references.

After the group's first anniversary, I began to take "minutes" at every gathering to create a narrative of that morning's festivities, which was then emailed to the group as part of the next weeks invite. These narratives then morphed into the posts for the Blog, "Breakfast with Dave" on wordpress.com.

This volume, highlighting posts from March 2011 to April 2012, is a 10th Anniversary tribute to the friendships, memories, and overall silliness that has become the backbone of 'Breakfast with Dave.' If a picture is indeed worth a thousand words, then here are 25 "snapshots" from the past that still resonate the mood and atmosphere of the table on that particular morning. At the same time, they also represent some of the more memorable moments in early 'Breakfast with Dave' history, not to mention that these pages also contain references to more than a few reputable places that offer a good breakfast.

So, would reading "The Best of BREAKFAST WITH DAVE, Vol. I" help solve the problems of the world?

NOT BLOODY LIKELY!

However, experiencing this book might be an amazingly zany tonic to help deal with them.

James V. Colubiale

TODAY'S SPECIALS

CLARY'S CORNER QUIPS

03/24/11

Cape May Court House, NJ: For April's first 'Breakfast with Dave', the entourage gathered once again at Clary's Country Corner Restaurant at Hereford Rd. and Rt. 9. Sending their regrets for this week were Ed Sherretta, who is still in Italy searching for the ultimate pasta, and Doug Letterman, who is in North Carolina camping out with the Full Moon Bus Club. Attending this week's gathering were Jim Colubiale, John Wilsey, Eddie Jurewicz, Steve Riley, Dave Smith and Paul Mathis. This week's special surprise guest was none other than Bernie Bischoff, who retired from Lower Cape May nearly 15 years ago! 'Mien Heir', as we would kiddingly call him back then, was in the area opening his shore home, heard about 'Breakfast with Dave', and thought he would sit in on this week's mayhem.

The Clary's Country Corner breakfast menu features all the facets of a complete breakfast and at unbelievably low prices. Two eggs, two pancakes and two pieces of breakfast meat costs, you guessed it, $2.22! (Monday through Friday, before 10 AM). In fact, Dave once again felt that THIS was the best omelet he has eaten. At any rate, Clary's wide and varied range of breakfast options and the more-than-fair prices will draw the group back here repeatedly. When living on a fixed income, Clary's is a godsend!

Bernie arrived somewhere between pre-breakfast coffee cups #2 and #3, and took us by surprise, thanks in large part to a tight-lipped Dave, who had always wanted 'Breakfast with Dave' to be like the Dean Martin show where every week another "guest" comes unannounced through his door. After we all reacquainted ourselves with how great we all looked, we immediately launched the conversation into the past, reminiscing about principals we have known and how none of them were very physically imposing. Not that this mattered to us, but it did provide Dave a great lead-in to a story from his Lenape years. While returning to their car after an event at the high school, a gang confronted Dave and his small group trying to sucker anyone to hit one of the gang members just to create an excuse to beat up Dave's friends. Miraculously, Dave's group made it safely to their waiting car. Or so they thought. The gang then began to literally rock the car so violently that they nearly had it off the ground. Then, out of the nearby school building comes the principal, a massive man, holding a 2 X 4 in his bare hand as if it was a stick and demanded the gang disperse. They peeled away in every which direction to avoid any further confrontation with "The Man." As Dave said, not too many students wanted to be on this guy's wrong side.

We had a big, imposing man at Lower Cape May Regional, but he was a shop teacher, not a principal, and inside his 6'5", 300-pound frame beat the heart of a lamb. However, Tom Mount was imposing in other ways. He had incredibly quick and strong hands. He was able to place his hand under someone's open hand and then snatch a quarter out of the palm before the person could close his hand. Dave and Jim saw him do this to a very close friend of Bernie's, Bill Carr, right in the main hallway at Lower Cape May. Bill thought he had the quarter in his hand until Tom showed it to him. The look he made at his empty hand was beyond amazement.

The rocking car made Bernie ask about OLD SCHOOL, the band John, Jim and Eddie J play in because the last time he saw them was two summers ago, on a Thursday night at the Rusty Nail in Cape May, NJ when he came to hear the band play. Although the band has not rehearsed in months, John has cleaned out his garage for the group to use on Tuesday nights for rehearsals. In fact, Jim helped jump-start the task by pitching-in during the first two days of clean-up last week. As they opened box after box, John was discovering more and more stuff he did not even know he had. For example, in one box he found a wetsuit hood and gloves in their original packaging! John felt like it was Christmas! Anyway, we told Bernie that we are back rehearsing and will keep him posted as to where and when we might play this summer.

After breakfast, the conversation touched upon some political points as the group lamented the inability of politicians, in general, to work together toward the common good as opposed to being so self-serving. A budget deficit now into the trillions of dollars and the ever-widening gap between the rich and the middle and lower classes are all outgrowths of political greed. Even Bernie, a Vermonter, feels that even politicians like Vermont's Senator Sanders are only championing the middle class for their political benefit.

However, before all this sobered us from our caffeine, the server brought another round. Eddie J mentioned that if we wanted a good laugh, we should all see David Greene's *Pineapple Express* when it arrives because the film promises to be very funny. Eddie's suggestion turned us away from discussions of Government shutdowns or New Jersey Gov. Christie's Town hall meeting at the Cape May County Airport next week, and re-focused our attention on more critical issues, like telling some jokes.

While we figured out the bill, we decided to have a "joke-off" between Paul and Dave since this was our first April breakfast (April's first). Paul lost the coin toss and went first.

Paul told a joke about this group of monks who took a vow of silence except for one day out of every year when one of them could say one thing while at dinner. The first year of silence ended, and while the monks are sharing their meal, the head monk selects someone to speak. The chosen monk stands and shouts: "THIS FOOD IS SHIT!"

The next year at their meal, another monk is selected, and he rises and exclaims: "NO IT'S NOT; IT'S PRETTY GOOD!"

The third year at their meal, the leader picks yet another monk who stands up and screams: "I CAN'T TAKE THIS CONSTANT BICKERING!"

Then, Dave took his turn. Using coffee creamers as visual aids, Dave told the story of the worms in a church: "A minister decided that a little visual demonstration would add emphasis to his Sunday sermon. So, the Minister placed four worms into four separate jars. He placed the first worm into a container of alcohol. The minister placed the second worm into a container of cigarette smoke. He then placed the third worm into a container of chocolate syrup while he placed the fourth into a container of good clean soil. At the conclusion of the sermon, the Minister reported the following results: The first worm in alcohol was dead. The second worm in cigarette smoke was dead. The worm in the chocolate syrup was also dead. The fourth worm in good clean soil was alive. So, the minister asked the congregation, what did you learn from this demonstration? Maxine was sitting in the back, quickly raised her hand and said, 'As long as you drink, smoke and eat chocolate, you won't have worms! '" Dave should receive bonus points here because he remembered the joke!

The final tally per person was $9.00 that included a very gracious tip for our attentive and pleasant server who doubled as a photographer and snapped the picture at the top of the minutes. Once again, the food at Clary's was fabulous; the atmosphere down home and the good times did roll.

BLUE PLATE SPECIAL

North Cape May, NJ: The 'Breakfast with Dave' Thursday morning soiree stayed local and invaded the Blue Plate Diner (previously the Rainbow Ice Cream Parlor) at the intersection of Townbank and Bayshore Roads in North Cape May. Again, Eddie Jurewicz could not attend due to a therapy appointment for his shoulder, and Ed Sherretta sent his regrets because he and Betty will be in Italy for the next three weeks. However, John Wilsey, just back from Hawaii, Jim Colubiale, Paul Mathis and Dave Smith all managed to attend and were fortunate enough to be joined by a surprising newcomer to the weekly morning madness--Gene Sole.

Yes, the Lieutenant Colonel himself honored our group to break 'fast' with us! He came bearing an unopened bottle of Wild Turkey (Rare Breed) that graced the table throughout the meal. This bottle was the very same one that Sean Murphy, Paul Mathis, and Jim Colubiale gave Gene just before he left for his last combat tour in Iraq. Gene accepted the gift on the condition that the four of them would gather when he returned and drink from the bottle with him. Unfortunately, Gene is presently in remission from his fight with colon cancer and could no longer have any alcohol. Now, Gene would like to entrust the bottle to us. Paul and Jim graciously accepted the duty and kept the bottle in full view on the table, ready to pass it off as designer pancake syrup if hard pressed.

The Blue Plate Diner has a menu similar to its predecessor, offering many different omelets and various Monday through Friday specials, like two plate size pancakes and sausage for $4.99. Dave said that the Tuscany omelet was outstanding. Our server was charming and accommodating, even enduring Dave's comeback of "Which half do you have?" when she said she had a half-sister.

Once we were comfortably into our coffee, John Wilsey prodded Gene to tell an "IT'S NOT A SMALL WORLD; IT'S A BIG CAPE MAY" story based on his Iraq experience. When the military deployed Gene, the assistant High School principal in charge of discipline, to Iraq, a former LCMR student, who had enlisted upon graduation, was also sent to the same region. Knowing this, Gene threw his USMC- Lieutenant-Colonel weight around and arranged to see him at his base. Well, the moment Gene arrives to see him, he finds Pvt. Josh Senbertrand is sitting in an out-house. So, he had the Sgt. pound on the door and told him (in so many words) to get his butt out of there ASAP because a Lt. Col. wishes to speak to him! Nevertheless, the look on Josh's face when he realized who was standing in front of him must have been unbelievable to see. Gene then told him that he had come all this way to resolve a few unsettled issues from Josh's high school days. Nevertheless, that is precisely something Gene would do.

As we each settled into our breakfasts, we all wanted to hear from Johnny Tsunami since he was away for over 17 days paddling around in the North Shore with waves bigger than school buses rolling at him. According to John, surfing those Sunset giants was more nerve-wracking than living through the tidal wave that hit about three days into his stay. Just surviving in the surf like that must be quite a rush.

So, when John then asked the group if they had ever outrun a police chase, we all felt that this was a logical course for the conversation to take at this point. John recounted the time nearly 30 years ago when he pulled a Paul Newman and outmaneuvered a local patrol car on his motorcycle in-and-out-and-around the night streets of Cape May and West Cape May. Just as he arrived at the point in the story where he had safely serpentined his way home, stashed the bike out of sight and hide behind a door trying to avoid the floodlight of the patrol car that had just turned up his driveway, the group welcomed another unexpected guest. Bill Mastriana, an LCMR alum, and Captain Louis Russo came into the Blue Plate and stopped by to say "hi."

The sight of Lower Township Police Chief Bill Mastriana caught John in the floodlight of the moment, and he never did finish his great-escape story. But he did make sure they wouldn't hang around by telling Bill that Butch March wanted to know if he would like to practice the javelin with him some time soon. Since Gene did not understand John's allusion, Jim decided to tell him the story about how, during one Spring track practice, Bill and Butch were warming up by throwing the javelin tip first into the ground to practice their release. However, they decided to kick-it-up a notch and stood opposite of each other playing their version of 'chicken.' Yada, Yada, Yada… Butch did not flinch and took a javelin into his in-step! At a future breakfast, someone should have Jim tell the sequel to this called, "Butch in the Emergency Room!"

As we washed down the last of the eggs, pancakes and omelets with round after round of coffee, Gene remarked that he had to get going. As he was leaving, Dave asked him to say hi to his kids for him. At which point, Gene challenged Dave to name his two sons. Dave went 50%, missing on Tyler, the one he should remember.

Tyler is now a senior and heading to the University of Florida, but when he was about 5, Gene, an assistant LCMR soccer coach, brought him to the pre-Middle Township night-soccer match carbo loading (spaghetti) diner at Jim's house. At one point, Dave wanted to know what the boy's name was and asked Gene who said, "Steve" with no hesitation at all. Therefore, for the rest of the afternoon, Dave was calling Tyler "Steve," and "Steve" was not answering. Dave spoke a little louder until "Steve" showed some response. Just as we were about to leave, Dave solemnly goes over to Gene and pulling him aside says he seriously feels that Gene should have "Steve's" ears checked because he's been talking to the boy all night, and he's only responding to a loud voice. To which Gene simply replies, "Maybe if you would call him by his real name, he'll respond." Then he said, "Come on, TYLER." Tyler stood up, and he followed us to the game.

When we finally asked for the check, the final tally for four was $12 each, which included a decent tip and Gene's meal. The food at the Blue Plate was delicious, filling and economical; the servers were prompt and courteous, and the memories shared will be embracing and long-lasting. Semper Fi.

RETURN TO YOUTH AT THE
BELLA VIDA GARDEN CAFE

4/7/11

West Cape May, NJ: For this sunny May Thursday morning, the 'Breakfast with Dave' entourage followed the flight of the gull and returned to Broadway in West Cape May at the Bella Vida Garden Cafe. In attendance for a little egg, grits and grins were Jim Ridgeway (aka J9r), John "Tsunami" Wilsey, Doug "The Calculator" Letterman (aka "D." Letterman), Dave "Shady Tree" Smith, Bill Noe, Wayne Mazurek, Ed Sherretta, Paul Mathis, Eddie Jurewicz and Jim Colubiale. The server, an ex-student from Lower Cape May Regional High School, began seating the group at a large table by the main entrance and remarked that we were all playing hooky from school. Jim retorted, "Yeah, they call it retirement now."

The Bella Vida Garden Cafe continues to offer an extensive range of breakfast offerings, and although the menu does have all the standard breakfast fare covered, the omelet selection is quite encompassing. In fact, the special for this Thursday morning was an omelet that featured hot spicy Italian sausage, red peppers, mushrooms and Swiss cheese which proved to be a very satisfying selection for several of the group. In addition, a breakfast goer can replace home fries with some of the best grits around. Bella Vita also serves Costa Rican coffee that has always been a strong draw for a contingent of caffeine freaks like us retired schoolteachers.

After our attentive server placed our orders and the first round of coffee or tea settled over the table, Jim Ridgeway made mention of his alma mater, Trenton State College. This mention caught the attention of Eddie Jurewicz who wanted to finally thank J9r for his bogus directions that caused Eddie and his group to be late to hear (and see) Kurt Vonnegut, Jr. at Trenton State over a decade ago. He had brought his copy of *Cat's Cradle* with him so that he could go backstage and maybe had Vonnegut sign his book. However, after their late arrival and some security issues, the guards denied them access to Mr. Vonnegut after the show. However, Eddie's determination and persistence would pay off in an autograph. Eddie patiently waited in the lobby and managed to speak with Vonnegut's son who had come out into the outside hallway. Recognizing him, Eddie asked if he would bring his dad his copy of *Cat's Cradle* and sign it for him. The son agreed, and Eddie watched as Kurt Vonnegut himself gave Eddie a thumbs up after he signed his book.

Then, as Jim Ridgeway was relating his "I-wanted-to-change-the-world" college experience of touring the Trenton State Prison, our attentive server brought breakfast to the table, just as he began to describe how they made license plates. Nevertheless, the whole experience scared him straight–-to the nearest bar! Almost as a pre-meal benediction, Paul mentioned that this past Tuesday (5/10) was National Monty Python Day. This announcement triggered an avalanche of favorite bits including "I'm a Lumber Jack and I'm OK," the Dead Parrot routine, the Internationale Philosophie Soccer match between the Greeks and the Germans (a favorite of Jim and Dave), and the entire *Holy Grail* film! Not to forget *Spam-a-lot*! After the group paid significant homage, eating began in earnest.

In between munching on eggs, omelets and French toast, Dave asked if anyone picked the winner in the 137th running of the Kentucky Derby last Saturday. As we would expect, Jim Ridgeway bet on the 20-1 shot, Animal Kingdom, and won! However, according to Ridgeway, the real story may be about how the police found Michael Baze, the jockey who rode Nehro to a second-place finish, dead in his car on the Tuesday following the event. Although the newspapers suggest that no apparent signs of foul play were evident, the whole situation sounds a bit suspicious.

Sometimes second is just not enough. Then, Dave challenged everyone to last night's Final Jeopardy question: "Which town hosts an annual major sporting event and has the word 'sport' in its name?" After several misfires from various table members, Jim Ridgeway came up with the answer: Williamsport, PA, home of the Little League World Series. This answer sent everyone back to those glorious days of Little League Baseball. Ed Sherretta was one of the charter members of the Cape May Little League back in the late 50's early 60's. He pointed out that the city located the first Little League ballpark where the Cape May Elementary School now has its parking lot. The deal was that when the city built the school, they would relocate the baseball field. So, they moved the park to its present location just down the street from the school on Lafayette Street in Cape May.

As we began to share our rural and urban Little League experiences, an elderly man walked by the table and kiddingly remarked that the town should have a statute about having so much fun at breakfast. And we continued to explain how Dave is a member of the Mayor's advisory committee and that we will have Dave bring this up at the next City Council meeting.

Meanwhile, Bill didn't know all this background about Dave, so Dave explained, in three-part harmony, how the mayor appointed him to the Cape May Shade Tree Commission and then, when he tried to resign the commission, the mayor would not let him and appointed him instead to his advisory committee. Bill was also impressed to discover that while Dave was with the Shade Tree Commission, the group has planted over 100 trees in the town of Cape May! Nobody ever said Dave does not get things done; he just does not do meetings.

As our server poured the final rounds of coffee and tea, the conversation snaked its way back to those "younger," carefree days of kick-the-can, buck-buck, hide-the-belt, or running in the wake of the Mosquito spray truck. We all did it, and with what we now know about those chemicals, we cannot believe that we did. Ed Sherretta was lamenting how the older people in his Cape May neighborhood were always out to get the kids who were playing ball near their property. When boys would hit a ball into their yards, they would keep the ball as a form of harassment. Meanwhile, Jim pointed out that in his South Philly street, if the old ladies did not want kids playing in front of their stoop, they would come out and throw buckets of boiling water at them. Heck with keeping the ball! Then, at precisely 10:15 Dave made the first *Seinfeld* reference when he mentioned the 'cleavage' episode as he was trying to describe how lifeguards should never be caught staring at good looking girls but only take a casual 'glance' in her general direction.

Once the check arrived, The Calculator took over and assessed that we each owed 14 dollars for this week. The Bella Vida Garden Cafe once again produced a very delicious breakfast with timely and courteous service all at decent prices, which is why this establishment has become a 'Breakfast with Dave' favorite. As we were all kicking in our money, Eddie J mentioned that Irma McVey, a retired colleague who has an inoperable cancerous brain tumor, was home and was welcoming visitors. So, we decided to adjourn to Irma's house in Erma and say HI to a dear old friend and thank her for the breakfasts she shared with us in her library office for so many years. Now, 'Breakfast with Dave' will continue this tradition.

STEVE'S DIRTY DOZEN

4/28/201

Dias Creek, NJ: The Thursday morning breakfast soiree, otherwise known as 'Breakfast with Dave', descended upon Steve's Cafe 47 on Route 47 in the Dias Creek section of Middle Township to share some pancakes and eggs on the last Thursday in April. A record number of 12 attendees gathered this week: first-timers Henry Wiegel and Bill Carr joined Eddie Jurewicz (just back from France), Eddie Sherretta (just returned from three weeks in Italy), Paul Mathis, Jim Ridgeway, Jim Colubiale, Capt. Bill Garrison, Dave Smith, Doug "D." Letterman, John Wilsey, and Steve Riley. If one more person would have arrived, we planned to re-create da Vinci's "The Last Supper." Doug would earn the nod for the role of Jesus because he did play an archbishop once in MAME. Besides, he is the only one who has a beard.

Steve and Henry were the last two to arrive not so much because the directions challenged them, but because they parked next to each other in the designated meeting parking lot for 15 minutes before they fully recognized each other. Once they both took their places at the end of the table, breakfast officially began. Bill Garrison, who was once the head of the Physical Education Department at Lower Cape May Regional, observed that there were more Phys. Ed. Teachers at the table than at most of the meetings he held back at school!

Steve's Cafe 47 offers standard breakfast fares, including eggs every-which-way, pancakes, and meats. The menu offered a somewhat unusual, but delicious, version of 'Pigs in Blankets' which is an egg, bacon, and sausage each wrapped in individual pancakes for $5.95. We had to laugh because each time the waitress came back to the table, a few more people arrived. However, she handled the group's order with great poise and patience. What's more, she always kept the regular and decaf coffee coming throughout the meal. In fact, she was so attentive at the end of the meal, Jim Ridgeway refused another refill by saying if he had any more caffeine, he would be able to bench press the booth we were sitting in–with us in it!

While we waited for our orders, Ed Sherretta set out some venison jerky as an appetizer, which was very tasty. Dave used some slices on top of his omelet. In addition to our pre-breakfast starter, Steve Riley shared some photographs from his archives. One picture was of a very young, but still very stylish, Elton John taken at the Tower or some other Philadelphia venue back in the day. John, Jim, and Dave particularly liked the picture of a teenaged Steve standing next to his 10' Gordon and Smith long board. Then, Paul brought up the idea that since 'Breakfast with Dave' did not receive a Royal Wedding invitation, we should create our own "coat of arms" or a royal shield, as Kate Middleton needed to do to conform to tradition. Paul's vision is acorns and squirrels across a syrup-soaked pancake crest.

Once the waitress, with the help of some staff, served all of our meals, Bill Garrison suggested that we all pause for a moment of silent prayer for a very good friend and past-colleague as well as a past president of the Lower Cape May Regional Education Association, Irma McVey, who was undergoing preliminary testing for a brain tumor. We all wholeheartedly agreed and bowed our heads in prayer for Irma.

Once the group emerged from silence, conversations and eating began in full earnest. As various discussions crescendoed through the dining area, Bill Garrison leaned across to Jim and told him just to shut his eyes and try to listen to the conversations swirling around the table. Jim reported that he now knows the utter frustration of a real ADHD student who is unable to focus on one thing for any actual length of time because their brain cannot properly filter the constant bombardment of outside stimuli. With that said, an exact account of what the group discussed at the table would have to involve some out-body-experience.

One notable Jim Ridgeway story brought back memories of the old (or original) Playpen, a nightclub in Diamond Beach in Lower Township. He recounted a time that John Kay and Steppenwolf were to play at the Playpen, and as manager, he had to pay him for the concert. The usual procedure is to pay a percentage before the show and the balance afterward. However, John Kay showed up with a metal case handcuffed to his wrist and demanded all the money before the band took the stage. JR said considering how John Kay cleaned-up his life from the early years of his rock and roll career, he trusted in the seriousness that Kay projected concerning his new run at Rock and Roll. Meanwhile, Jim C. added that Steppenwolf was the very first concert he ever attended; he saw them at Villanova University in the early 70's.

Under the heading of "IT'S NOT A SMALL WORLD; IT'S A BIG CAPE MAY," Bill Carr offered the following story. He traveled to London once with his wife, and while they were in a London Pub, they bumped into a couple who sat on the beach with them every summer in Wildwood Crest. Adding to this "Small World" phenomenon, Paul mentioned that once his sister-in-law, while taking the tour of the Grand Canyon, met her one-time boss, Ross Simon, principal emeritus of Cape May Courthouse Elementary, at the bottom of the Grand Canyon.

Toward the end of breakfast, Smitty made the first reference to *Seinfeld* when he mentioned the 'bris' episode, which launched Paul into the following joke of the day: "A moil was cleaning out his desk after thirty years of service when his wife walks in and sees these slivers of skin in the drawer. When she asks her husband what they were, he tells her that they are the remains of all the bris ceremonies he had presided over. The wife would hear none of this and demanded that he remove them from the house immediately. Giving in, he gathered them up and was about to throw them out when he had an idea: "Why not make them into something I can keep with me?" So, he found a leather-worker and told him of his dilemma. The leather-worker said to come back in two days. When the man returned two days later, the leather-worker handed him a wallet. The man was amazed! "Wow!" He says, "This is great! How much do I owe you?" The leather-worker says, "$3,000.00." The man, incredulous, says, "$3,000.00 for a wallet?" The leather-worker replies, "It's not JUST a wallet. If you rub it, it will expand into a suitcase!"

As we waited for Doug to tally the bill, Eddie Jurewicz, who recently returned with Lynn Massimiano from visiting Strasbourg, France to see his son Chris (along with the Army of Freshman) perform at a local music festival, offered everyone an after breakfast piece of French chewing gum. The final bill came to be $10 each, which included a very gracious tip and two complimentary breakfasts for first timers, Bill Carr and Henry Wiegel. Although the food was delicious and the service outstanding, what made this week's 'Breakfast with Dave' so great was the experience of 12 retirees reuniting to rekindle old memories and deepen new friendships. ROCK ON!

TWO FOR ONE SPECIAL!

5/19/2011

Rio Grande, NJ:

See, here is what happens when key players take a hiatus from their usual routine…

Paul Mathis here, friends, with this week's installment of "Breakfast with Dave." Resident wordsmith (and co-founder) Jim Colubiale and his lovely spouse are out in Chicago (that toddlin' town) to visit their son, AJ, and attend his graduation from the School of the Art Institute's Masters Writing Program. In addition, Eddie J and his lovely spouse, Lisa, tooled up the AC Expressway to Camden to see their son, Brett, receive his Juris Doctorate from Rutgers University Law School. Congratulations go out to both families busting with pride at their offsprings' accomplishments. Well done, kids.

So, what happened? Well, Dave wanted to hang close to town because he wanted to deliver a rolling beach chair to our friend and former colleague, Irma Mc Vey, after breakfast. Since Irma lives in Erma (a cue for a ditty if there ever was one), Dave wanted to stay local, so the group deferred their original destination of Polly's in Stone Harbor to another date. He needed to contact everyone to announce the change in venue and came knocking on my office door Wednesday afternoon w/ those sad puppy dog eyes looking for assistance. We got the update out in time, and Thursday, May 19 found us all sitting around two large tables at the RIO GRANDE DINER in Rio Grande.

In attendance were Wayne Mazurek, Dave Smith, Bill Garrison, Bernie Bischoff, Bill Carr, Paul Mathis and Bill Noe who reminded all that the end of the world was scheduled to begin on Saturday. I am happy to report no one panicked.

Seeing both Bill and Bernie prompted Paul to extend greetings from Bernie and Bill's former science department chair at the high school, Jerry Gius. Bernie noted that Paul had already shouted out to Jerry earlier in the week with an email when he responded to Jim's previous blog with, "It's gold, Jerry. Gold!" Dave and Paul explained that Paul was not commenting to Jerry Gius, but rather referencing Banyon commenting to Jerry Seinfeld that his one-liners were the stuff of genius. Thus, the first SEINFELD reference of the morning came at just about 9:20.

Moments later Paul's cell phone rang. It was Jim calling from Chicago (that toddling' town). He and his lovely spouse, Debbie, had just landed and they were on their way to the hotel. He wanted to check in and let us know he was with us in spirit. The group exchanged greetings and after Jim hung up, we all agreed we would send him the check at meal's end.

When our ever-attentive server mentioned that she was from Greece, Bernie countered that he had just come back from a trip to the island of Minos in the Aegean off the coast. He chatted briefly with our server about his stay there, and they both agreed that the food and wine were hard to beat. We joked that she was going to take us all to her family's home in Greece on the tip we were going to leave her.

Eggs, omelets, home fries, bacon, scrapple, toast and cinnamon rolls soon piled high on the table and coffee flowed like rivers of black gold. Soon Dave mentioned Altoona, Pennsylvania, which lit up Bill Carr's eyes. Seems Bill went to college out in Altoona and besides his stellar education in the life sciences, he remembered quite fondly several young ladies studying for their degrees in nursing. We all agreed that we now wanted to become doctors and Dave admitted that he only brought the subject up because he liked saying the word, "Altoona". He did admit, however, to a certain fondness for nurses himself. He had actually thought of becoming a dentist at one point, but he did not want to spend all his days looking down in the mouth.

About this time, a woman came over to the table and was very happy to see all of us. Bill Noe immediately recognized her as one of the women who used to work in the cafeteria at Teitelman. After we shared the usual amenities, someone referred to Teitelman's legendary moniker of "Big T". This prompted Wayne to set the record straight.

It seems that several decades ago, the district hired a young woman to teach in the district, and her vital statistics did not go unnoticed by several of the men on staff, particularly Bill Porter and Jack Donaldson. Now, knowing the late Bill Porter and Jack Donaldson, we all knew neither Bill nor Jack was likely to let this particular observation die a natural death. Apparently, one morning in the presence of the principal, Bill asked Jack how "Big T" was doing, and the principal thought Bill was asking about their school, the Richard M. Teitelman Junior High School. She liked how appropriately the moniker fit, made it her own and to this day the school is often referred to as "Big T", even though originally "Big T" had nothing to do with junior high school and everything to do with…aw, forget it.

Remembrances of Bill and Jack, both wrestling coaches at one time, prompted Dave to question why wrestling weigh ins are no longer conducted in the nude. In order to get an accurate weigh-in, and since weight class strictly determines wrestling divisions, athletes had to step up on the scale naked. Those familiar with the procedure said that today's athletes weigh in wearing skivvies. Seems the NJSIAA received complaints from someone with enough power to change the regulation. Mention of Jack Donaldson prompted Dave to relate a somewhat unbelievable story about Jack, high school wrestling and watching an athlete make weight.

The story goes that Jack witnessed a weigh-in where a young man was one ounce over the limit for his weight class. Jack overheard the boy's coach tell him to go over in the corner and stand on his head. The kid went over to the corner and stood on his head for a few minutes. When he returned to the scale, the extra ounce did not register, and the kid made weight. Bill, Bernie, and Bill Carr were suspicious of the practice, but Dave insisted that Jack witnessed the whole event. We decided the next time we could no longer fit into those favorite jeans we would try standing on our heads to see if it helped at all.

Bill Noe again reminded us that Saturday was the Rapture and asked if we had made plans for the end of the world, as we knew it. Most folks just dismissed the idea, but Paul said he had a good vantage point on the roof, enough shrimp to fill a barbie, several bottles of Jefferson Reserve Single Barrel bourbon, and his copy of The Band's THE LAST WALTZ on an iPod. Overall, it seems Paul is best prepared for the end of the world, as we know it.

The bill came to $11 each, and all agreed it was a fine meal.

As we left the diner, Bernie, Bill and Paul noticed an unusual automobile parked across the street next to Dunkin' Donuts. It was an older faded red sports car and looked something like an old Studebaker Avanti. Upon closer inspection, it turned out to be a Zimmer. Its long lines and extremely modest height were impressive. The rooftop is mid-thigh in height.

Our missing brethrens' absence was noted, but it was good to see Bernie and Bill Carr again.

As a post script, we all stopped at Irma's in Erma to help her get into the chair Dave had provided, but her daughter, Diane, met us outside and said she wasn't seeing visitors that morning as her spirits weren't as good as we might have hoped. We sent our regrets and well wishes by proxy and hope to see Irma next week.

Quod erat demonstrandum

The good times rolled.

"Thanks for the use of the hall."

-Paul

Meanwhile, in Chicago…

Chicago, Illinois: Since Jim was in Chicago visiting his son AJ, who happens to be the administrator/editor of the 'Breakfast with Dave' blog-site, he thought that hosting a 'Breakfast with Dave' splinter-group gathering with him as part of his visit would be fitting. So, Jim, his wife Debbie, his son AJ and his girlfriend Kelly walked south down Michigan Avenue from the Congress Hotel for breakfast at Yolk.

The Yolk's menu goes well beyond the standard breakfast fare of eggs any-which-way or fruit laden waffles and pancakes, offering several freshly squeezed breakfast fruit juices and some very tasty "scramblers" which are actually scrambled eggs mixed with at least two or three other ingredients, like bacon and/or cheese. They also make their own coffee, which was continually re-filled throughout the breakfast by the more than attentive staff.

After we placed our orders and had our first sips of the Yolk blended coffee, the conversation quickly re-focused on a major adjustment that a Cape May visitor must make while visiting a large city like Chicago, which is dealing with the homeless who sometimes line the sidewalk at twenty-five foot intervals. One such individual greeted us as we entered the establishment, and he was there to say good-bye, as well.

Debbie had a story about how her sister Barbara would deal with such people. Debbie said that one day her sister Barbara was driving through Medford, NJ and saw a destitute Spanish looking woman in the middle of the street holding a sign asking for money and food. She pulled over and then proceeded to yell at the women saying that she cannot beg like that in the middle of the street. Although the lady spoke very little English, she managed to successfully communicate that she had just lost her job, and she had no husband to support her and her daughter, and had very little food, if any, to feed her child. Barbara, who cannot speak any Spanish, coaxes the lady to go with her to the super market where the lady can select some staples for herself and her child, and she (Barbara) would pay for them even though Barbara's husband had been out of work for many months and times were hard for the Meckles. When the woman returns to the checkout aisle, her cart is full of cigarettes and laundry detergent, electric toothbrushes, top-shelf Tampons, etc. Well, Barbara, calls for a person named Pedro who obviously speaks the language and commands him to tell the woman to put all that back and buy FOOD. When the woman returns to the checkout aisle, she now has about $60 dollars' worth of milk, bread, eggs, juice, ground meat and some peanut butter and jelly. As the cashier was bagging the groceries, the lady turns to Barbara and says that she really doesn't know what she's going to do with these groceries because she has no money to pay the rent at her apartment and will have nowhere to put them. Unbelievably, she then asked if Barbara would be kind enough to give her money for her rent as well! Barbara then launched into a tirade that, to this day, remains intertwined with Ralphie's Dad's rants against the furnace in *The Christmas Story* somewhere over Lake Michigan.

As soon as the food arrived, AJ offered a toast to acknowledge the 700th hit on the 'Breakfast with Dave' blog site. Kelly remarked that she visits and enjoys reading about our conversations. However, she was curious to know how this weekly event was first set in motion. So, Jim thought that this was as good as any other time to try and remember how this all came together.

'Breakfast with Dave' started sometime in the fall of '09 with e-mail from Dave to Jim stating simply: "How about breakfast?" Jim contacted Paul to see if he wished to be included. His emailed response became the inspiration for our little group's name, "Breakfast with Dave? I'm in!" Once we dropped the question mark, "Breakfast with Dave" was born.

We agreed to meet at the now defunct Bella Magiatta on Bayshore Road in the Villas, NJ. We had such a tremendous time that we agreed that as long as two of the group can make the gathering, we will have a breakfast together every Thursday morning at various eateries around the Cape May County area at 9 AM. The first several breakfasts were proverbial joke contests. In fact, AJ, himself, participated at one held over Christmas break '09. By the summer of '10 Eddie J began as a regular and from there our numbers swelled as word spread to those colleagues who preceded us as well as followed us into retirement.

As we washed down a delicious breakfast with one last cup of their delectable fresh brewed coffee, Jim quickly figured the bill just to compare the cost to back home. The individual cost for this breakfast was $14.00/per., which included a very nice tip for the very attentive and pleasant staff. All in all, Yolk was a very fine choice for a Chicago edition of 'Breakfast with Dave." That's no Yolk… (I just had to say that)

TUCKAHOE FAMILY DINER:
THE UN-PET-ABLES

6/9/2011

Woodbine, NJ: On this unbelievably hot and humid June Thursday morning, the 'Breakfast with Dave' traveling breakfast symposium journeyed to Woodbine to visit the landmark Tuckahoe Family Diner on Route 50 in Woodbine. This lone diner, which may be the last of the actual boxcar type diners left in the area, actually had a Petting Zoo in the back! Even though we could have sat all together on the Grapevine covered veranda, we opted for the inside air-conditioned comfort of two separate booths and the counter stools.

Braving the heat and humidity this Thursday to share some food, fun and memories were: Henry Weigel, 'Birthday Boy' Bill Noe, first-timer Ray MacAlarnan, Paul Mathis, Eddie Jurewicz, and Jim Colubiale. Also, a surprise 'Breakfast with Dave' guest attended, direct from a two year MFA stint at the School of the Art Institute of Chicago, AJ Colubiale, administrator and editor of the "Breakfast with Dave" blog site. He came to revisit the 'Breakfast with Dave' phenomenon in this rarest of venues.

The inside of the diner teleported us back into time. We were waiting to hear Rod Sterling's voice telling us we are now in the Twilight Zone. Decorated with real forty-five records (remember them?) hanging from the ceiling, and actual poster ads for products, like Coke-a-Cola or Chevy, literally plaster the walls. The server even wears a real poodle skirt! The menu offers all the essential breakfast ingredients like eggs, omelets, pancakes and French toast with assorted side meats as well. However, Dave will attest that his omelet was one of the best he's had in a while. Two eggs any style, two pieces of meat and two pancakes (or French toast), was only $5.95. In addition, the coffee and tea were bottomless and great tasting.

Before we could even swallow our first sips of coffee, Dave plops a "WARNING" citation on the table that a State Trooper slapped him with while on his way up the Parkway. Dave then proceeds to tell us that a State Trooper was passing him when suddenly the patrol car slowed and pulled in back of Dave's car, eventually pulling him over. The trooper then told Dave that he pulled him over for driving while talking on his cell phone. Dave explained that he did not even have a cell phone with him and that he just had his hand by his ear. Then Jim butted in and asked if there was any "penetration" into the ear, and 'Breakfast with Dave'

had its first *Seinfeld* reference at 9:07 AM alluding to the infamous "nose pick" episode. The trooper believed him (we guess) but issued him a warning for a burnt out tail light anyway.

As the server took our orders, Dave asked about the Petting Zoo, and she told him that they had to close the Zoo because of their inability to keep up with all the new legal requirements for running such an operation. When a dejected Dave asked what happened to all the animals, the waitress explained that they sold them to various Zoos and circuses or some they kept as pets. Paul remarked that he knew, beforehand, the Petting Zoo was closed. He'd planned to bring a goat to breakfast tied up in the back of his Ford Ranger pick-up truck for Dave to pet in an attempt to assuage Dave's disappointment about the Zoo closure. However, the heat 86ed that idea.

When the waitress mentioned the Zoo had several monkeys, Henry pointed out that he once had two spider monkeys, King Kong and Maggie Mae, for many years while he was working with us at the Erma School of Hard Knocks. When Dave asked Henry what life was like with two monkeys around the house, Henry offered a tale. Henry had Kong on top of his head one day when he and his pre-teen daughter entered into an argument over some arrangements for the upcoming weekend. Well, as the voices elevated, Kong became more and more agitated. Henry then informed the group that when spider monkeys get this way, they not only clamp down onto their perch, in this case, his head, but they suffer from diarrhea as well. So, Henry suffered a spider monkey shampoo! After that, we all got the picture that spider monkeys do not make good household pets.

Once the server brought our food from the kitchen, Paul asked if anyone had seen the Soupy Sales documentary the other night on the New Jersey Network. Immediately, Jim started to rattle off the characters on the show: White Fang, Black Tooth, Pookie and the Pookie Players along with Hippie the hippo. Dave remembered the time they had the naked girl outside the door as a surprise guest when Soupy would routinely check to see who was at the door at the end of each show. If we all were not so engrossed with our food, we would have jumped up and did the "The Mouse" in the aisles! Paul pointed out that Uncle Floyd (Floyd Vivino) paid tribute to Soupy Sales in the Documentary. Uncle Floyd was one of the many performers that Eddie J brought to the stages of Lower Cape Maybe Regional for the community's benefit and enjoyment. In fact, Jim has an exceptional memory of that night because his then pre-teen Vince went up on stage, along with Eddie J's son, Brett, to be a part of a band that Uncle Floyd was putting together. After Vince selected the wash-board for his instrument, Floyd asked him if he knew how to play it.

When Vince confidently responded that he did, Floyd asked, "What, are you poor?"

As the server bused the tables, Bill circulated a picture of him with Jim O'Neil, a past principal of the high school, now a Superintendent at a school in Chatham. The photo inspired Bill to tell a story of how O'Neil took a State inspector out to his "garage" classroom to look it over. Due to limited classroom space in the school building, Bill, who would drink his morning coffee from a lab beaker, was allowed (along with Karl Toft) to set up his Earth Science/Marine Biology class room in an old garage outside the school. The room had a look and the feel of something out of Steinbeck's *Cannery Row*, with fish tanks, cages, and sea artifacts encircling the desk area. When O'Neil arrived at the room, Bill was up on the roof administering to the class' weather station. However, since the inspector came to see how Bill operated his lab, Bill insisted that both O'Neil and the inspector climb up on the roof with him so that he could clarify how things worked. However, before Bill could explain what makes the wind blow, the inspector excused himself, and Bill never had another inspection. Bill just dazzled him with science!

Then, Bill informed the gathered congregation that today was his 69th birthday, and, as a real researcher, he proceeded to cite other notable figures who shared his birthdate, like Jerry Garcia and Paul McCartney. He even pointed out that the potato chip was named a food on this day back in the 50's, which caused Jim to remind the gang that the Federal health department has officially abandoned the "Food Pyramid" in favor of a "Food Plate" because too many Americans were starting to look like pyramids! We all wished Bill a very Happy Birthday and also hoped that he has an even greater "Summer of '69".

Once the bill arrived and we began to figure out what we each owed for the meal, we had one more piece of business to settle before we adjourned until next week. Over the last two weeks, Jim has received two e-mails from a person who wants to buy the domain name, "breakfastwithdave.com." The last correspondence suggested that he call to discuss the possibility of a sale, so after breakfast, Jim did just that and spoke to the man while the collective mayhem of 'Breakfast with Dave' droned in the background. The bottom line is that "breakfastwithdave.com" is not for sale, and Jim thanked the man for his interest.

The final individual tab for this week's meal was $10.00 which (as usual) included a substantial tip for our very informative and attentive poodle-skirted waitress. The food was excellent, and the good times were even better. All in all, The Tuckahoe Family Diner's nostalgic atmosphere proved to be the perfect setting for this week's stroll down memory lane.

ANECDOTES AND OMELETS: ON THE BEACH AT MCGLADE'S

6/16/2011

Cape May, NJ: McGlade's Restaurant on the Pier along the Cape May promenade was the setting for this last Spring Thursday's 'Breakfast with Dave' morning soiree and anecdote symposium. This week, Lynn Massimiano, Doug "D" Letterman, Paul Mathis, Capt. Bill Garrison, Eddie Jurewicz, Jim Colubiale were joined by special guests AJ Colubiale, the administrator/editor of the 'breakfastwithdave.wordpress.com' blog site, and his love-interest from Chicago, Kelly Sheehy for some omelets and merriment. In addition, a surprise guest from Alaska, Dave's boyhood friend from Medford, NJ, Jim Klauder, literally strolled in a bit late and made himself right at home before Barney introduced him to the group. By the way, since Dave's lifeguard duties kept him from attending 'Breakfast with Dave", he sent his "second", Barney, to sit in for him.

McGalde's, situated right on the beach next to the gaping hole that once was and hopefully once again will be Cape May's Convention Hall, offers a tremendous line- up of omelets, specializing in seafood omelets. Besides offering tremendous ocean front dinning views, all the meals are also garnished deliciously with fresh fruit. Eggs and Waffles are also offered for those not of the omelet mind- set. Even so, not having an omelet at McGlade's is like going to the boardwalk and not riding the roller coaster.

As the group settled into their first of several cups of coffee, the discussion shifted quickly from how the Boston Bruins bullied their way to the Stanley Cup, to how the Phillies are presently living up to all their preseason hype, to the nature of various nicknames. Barney mentioned that Dave wanted his grandchildren to call him "Zeus", but when the kids try to say "Zeus", it comes out "Wooeus" instead. But even Jim K. said it sounds cute because it does "fit" Dave. This discussion led to a mention of the new "children's" book by Adam Mansbach called, *Go the F^#k to Sleep*, which is all the rage on YouTube these days read by Samuel L. Jackson.

After our orders were taken, Paul, who loves flamingoes and arrived a little late this week to hear all the introductions, wanted to know if this was the friend from Alaska who would set up pink flamingo lawn ornaments along a short stretch of the Iditarod dog sled race course every year. And indeed, he is the very same one! So the group began to snowball him with questions and suggestions about Sara Palin's possible second run for the Presidency. As if to demonstrate how someone like Palin can rise to such political heights from Alaska, Jim K. told a story of how up-in-arms the Alaskans are over Oil Company taxes. However, when the Oil Companies attempted to appeal to the Alaskan people by offering an 18% tax on oil instead of the 20% tax they had originally intended on imposing, the Alaskans, instead of negotiating for an even lower tax, just blindly jumped at the offer with no further negotiations to lower the tax level. This was like Kramer quickly accepting the Coffee Shop's offer of free coffee and lattes for life without waiting to hear that they also were prepared to offer $50,000 as well. And so, we had our first *Seinfeld* connection at 9 AM.

Once our server delivered our meals, the group needed to "rearrange" the plates a bit so that everyone received their correct omelet. As the plates were moving around, Jim C. reminded the group of the last time this occurred here at McGlade's. Dave and Paul ordered different omelets almost a year ago to the day. Dave went for the salt, but the salt was not coming out well enough, so Dave removed the top. However, Dave failed to re-tighten the lid well enough, and when Paul went to put salt on his omelet, the top fell off and nearly the whole shaker emptied onto his breakfast. Dave thought this was very funny, and as poor Paul was trying to scrap the excess salt off his food, Dave tastes a bit of his omelet and remarks that it is delicious but not what he had ordered. Then, Paul opened his a bit and realized that **he** had Dave's and then swapped with him, leaving Dave with the sodium omelet. Anyway, once everyone had their respective meals, we all settled into our food.

In between bites and swallows, Lynn asked Jim K if he owned any sled dogs, and Jim K answered that he did indeed have a team of 8 dogs which he kept not so much for racing but for general transportation from time to time. This led Jim to tell of his first job in his new Alaskan home. When he first arrived there, he meets a person who owned 60 sled dogs and hired him to help "take care of the dogs". This included shoveling the dog's shit every day, which eventually became a full time job unto itself!

As the meal was winding down and the third and fourth rounds of coffee were circulating the table, Jim C. mentioned that he had yet more business to discuss with the group. Just the other day, a LCMR alumnus named Ben called Jim C to ask whether or not 'Breakfast with Dave' would be interested in letting him host a Thursday soiree for the gang. The purpose for all this would be to allow Ben and his financial consulting group to pitch their services to this particular gaggle of retirees. Upon hearing this news, the group all agreed that they would have a very hard time taking the whole presentation seriously, and as if to reinforce this idea, Jim K told a story about what his father and Dave's dad did to a Kirby Vacuum salesman during a "demonstration" at their former Medford home.

After accepting a telephone appointment for the Kirby Vacuum salesman to come to Jim K's house in Medford, The Smith's and the Klauder's organized a very elaborate and detailed plan to simply drive the salesman crazy. After the salesman arrived, they allowed him to set up his demonstration in the living room. Once he was about 5 minutes into his spiel, a woman knocks at the door and asks if she can use their washer because hers in not working, so she enters the house. The Kirby guy is just about back into his pitch, when the doorbell rings again. This time a young man tells Jim K's dad that he is working his way through college and wanted to know if he was interested in a magazine subscription. Mr. Klauder politely says that he is sorry, but he really did not want to subscribe to anything at that time but asked him whether he would like to come in and ask the Kirby guy if he could work for his company selling vacuum cleaners. While Mr. Klauder is making all the necessary introductions, another woman (from the neighborhood) comes to the door asking to use their dryer because hers is on the brink. She also enters the house. Again the Kirby Rep. starts his demo one more time, only to be interrupted again by a gentleman who wishes to speak to the first woman who came in to do her wash. While the Kirby guy is trying to run the vacuum over the rug to show how much more dirt it can pick up over their vacuum, the man loudly tells the washer lady that she just hit the lottery for $15,000 dollars! As the entire house now begins to celebrate, the Kirby salesman is sucked into the gaiety (the woman said that now she too would buy a Kirby Vacuum) and does not notice our own Jim K, who is only 8 to 10 years old at the time, slowing pouring sand out of his pocket onto the vacuumed rug. When the Kirby man resumes his demonstration vacuuming, all this sand is pulled up from a rug that should have been clean from the first pass.

Trying to conceal his confusion over all this, the Kirby guy tells the gathered throng that one of the many attachments that comes with the vacuum is a sharpener. So, he asks if anyone had something they wanted sharpened. Mr. Smith said that he did and went across the street and brought over a real infantry bayonet. Although a little taken a-back with the request, the undaunted Kirby salesman starts to try and sharpen the bayonet. He doesn't get very far before the doorbell rings yet again and a man enters with a Kirby Vacuum and tells the salesman that he saw his car outside and thought that he could take a look at his vacuum cleaner because it just hasn't been working. Little did the Kirby guy know that the group had painted clear nail polish over the prongs, and so he too couldn't get the machine to work. However, he thought that the problem could be inside the machine and proceeded to dismantle the vacuum in the middle of the living room. While he was focused on fixing the "broken" Kirby, the group painted clear nail polish on the prongs of his vacuum. Then, in the middle of all this chaos, an unidentified man walks into the living room, pours himself a shot from a bottle of whiskey that has been up on the fireplace mantle all afternoon, slaps a dollar down on the mantle and leaves without so much as saying a word. Anxious to now finish the demonstration and get out of this mad house, the Kirby guy plugs in his Vacuum only to find that it too does not work. Totally flabbergasted, the poor Kirby vacuum salesman gathered up all the pieces of his vacuum and literally ran out of the house!

At this point, Doug "the calculator" interrupted the story to tell everyone that the individual total was $12.00. As the group was pooling their money to pay the waitress, Jim K mentions that his story has an epilogue of sorts. About 10 or so years later, after the Klauder's had left Medford, Mrs. Klauder had another Kirby salesman come to her door. When she remarked that she once had a demonstration given to her when she lived in Medford, the salesman's eyes bugged out, and he too literally ran away. The Medford Incident, as the escapade came to be known in the Kirby Vacuum sales world, had become legend! And with that, this 'Breakfast with Dave' will go down in the annals as another crazy and fun morning of good food and great tales.

COMING FULL CIRCLE AT
THE BACK BAY BISTRO

7/14/11

Villas, NJ: The 'Breakfast with Dave' traveling Thursday morning soiree continued its summer Lower Cape May Regional alumni tour by visiting the Back Bay Bistro and Pizzeria on Bayshore Road in the Villas section of Lower Township, which is owned and operated by LCMR alumnus Sherri Hemingway. This eatery holds a little 'Breakfast with Dave' history in that this was the site of the very first 'Breakfast with Dave' nearly two years ago when it was called Bella Mangiata, attended by charter members Dave Smith, Paul Mathis, and Jim Colubiale. Sherri has just opened the new eatery this past July 4th weekend, and the gang thought it would be a nice gesture to patronize an LCMR alumni's business. This time around, Doug "D" Letterman, Paul Mathis, Eddie Jurewicz, Jim Colubiale and Captain Bill Garrison were in attendance on this beautiful July summer morning. Bill Carr and John Wilsey sent their regrets for this week. Again, lifeguard Dave Smith was watching the waves and could not join in on the fun this week.

The Back Bay Bistro and Pizzeria's menu offer all the necessary ingredients for an excellent breakfast, such as eggs of any style as well as pancakes and French toast. An assortment of omelets rounds out the morning offerings along with a few specials, like a 2-2-2 breakfast of 2 eggs, two pancakes and two pieces of breakfast meat for $2.22 (before 9 AM) and a delicious Eggs Benedict for $6.95. Our waitress, Crystal, who is also an LCMR alumnus, kept the freshly brewed coffee coming throughout the meal.

Once the group settled into their table and had their first cups of coffee and tea, breakfast commenced with the "Dave Smith Story of the Week." Paul began with little vignettes of some of "Dave Smith's Greatest Hits." He began with a tale of Smitty coming into his class unannounced with an unraveled coat hanger and said to Paul in front of the class, "This wire just came for you!" Then Paul recounted the time Dave opened Paul's classroom door and rolled a penny across the front of the room. However, one of the most memorable incidents was the time the music department wanted to include the faculty in its Christmas concert for the student body and gathered together everyone who could play guitar to come up on stage and strum along to "Grandma Got Run Over by a Reindeer." In this group, which was the first faculty band, were Paul Mathis, Doug Letterman and Jim Colubiale of the 'Breakfast with Dave' contingent as well as Jackie Mcknew, Sunny Palmer, Steve Leadley and a host of others. Dave wanted to join in on the fun as well, even though he didn't play guitar, so he walked out on stage with a red scarf around his neck wearing sunglasses while pretending to play a stand-up bass he borrowed from the music room. He brought the house down.

Eddie J. followed up Paul's story with one that not only connected to Dave but also to the 'Breakfast with Dave' slogan of "IT'S NOT A SMALL WORLD; IT'S A BIG CAPE MAY." Many years ago, Eddie went to Nashville to visit the Steinberger factory where he met a man named Jeff. When Eddie told him that he was from Cape May and worked at Lower Cape May Regional, Jeff asked him if he knew Dave Smith, and said they were terrific friends for many years. Jeff then proceeded to tell Eddie of a time when the two of them went to New York to see Woody Allen perform at a club and an unidentified man in a trench coat walked up to the stage with a bag in his hand. When he emptied the bang on the stage, all that came out was a pair of chattering teeth. So, Woody Allen then did about a 20-minute ad lib on the teeth.

As our food arrived and the gang began to enjoy their meals, Paul mentioned to Jim that he has been in contact with Jim's eldest son Vince via Facebook trying to calm him down about the current debt situation and the problems our government is having coming to a consensus with the debt ceiling. Jim asked whether Vince listed himself as in a 'relationship' or not because he is presently dating a beautiful and intelligent girl named Katie. Paul responded that he was not sure what Vince's posted status, but Jim stressed that "independent" Vince now no longer exists. Worlds have collided! Thus, we had our 'Breakfast with Dave' *Seinfeld* connection for the morning at about 9:45. Then Doug provided a little history by pointing out that under then President Bush, the debt ceiling was raised at least three times in his eight-year reign. The last time of the three, then Sen. Obama voted against raising the ceiling. And now, the Republicans are making him pay for that by fighting his proposals on this issue. Paul commented that the group's mutual friend Jerry summed up this situation best when he said, "If Obama sneezed and pulled out a handkerchief, the GOP would say he is against the tissue industry!"

Once the server bused the plates from the table, we all sat back to enjoy yet another round of coffee and tea. Eddie asked if anyone watched the All-Star Game Home Run Derby and saw that man who nearly fell 20 feet trying to catch one of the home run balls. The fans surrounding him saved his life by grabbing his legs and pulling back over the rail. This would have been a horrible repeat of what happened just a week before in Houston when a man fell 20 feet to his death attempting to catch a foul ball. The reference to this incident triggered a whole "foul ball story" time which included the time a man caught a foul ball at a Phillies game and then gave it to his five-year-old daughter who then promptly threw the ball back on the field. The man was stunned, but he did nothing but hug his little girl. We all agreed that he deserved an "A" as a father. Then, another time one boy caught two consecutive foul balls in a row. What would be the odds of that happening? Finally, Jim offered a story about a time when his dad took him to Connie Mack Stadium in Philadelphia to see the Phillies play the San Francisco Giants. Jim, who must have been 10 or 11 at the time, had the chance of seeing Willie Mays play in that game and had seats in the lower level along the first base line right about where the stands began to bend to meet the right-field wall. Willie McCovey sent a screaming line drive right at them, and Jim's dad rose to his feet to try and bare-hand the ball. He reached out over the row in front of him, but McCovy hit the ball with such force that the pain kept his father from closing his hand around the ball, which then plopped down in the lap of the guy sitting in front of him. Jim's dad's hand was swollen, and black and blue for days! Switching back to the All-Star Game, Eddie wanted to know if everyone had a chance to see Matt Szczur, a Chicago Cub's draftee and a 2008 graduate of Lower Cape May Regional, play in the futures All-Star game on ESPN this past Sunday night. Eddie reminded everyone that when he retired, Matt autographed the cork- board in his classroom. Now that autograph may soon be worth something. So, we all pledged that we would one day sneak back into the school, ninja-like, and cut out the signature before someone unknowingly paints over it.

Once the check arrived, Doug "the Calculator" figured that each of us owed $9.00 for this 'Breakfast with Dave' soiree, which we all agreed was quite reasonable. The food was delicious; the portions were more than filling and the service was prompt and gracious. Everything about the Back Bay Bistro & Pizzeria suggested that 'Breakfast with Dave' had indeed come home.

DAVE'S NOT HERE!

7/28/11

Cape May, NJ: For this last July Thursday, the 'Breakfast with Dave' moveable morning feast and soiree extravaganza visited the elegantly Victorian Aleathea's Restaurant located at the corner of Ocean and Beach Drives in Cape May. Even from the main dining room, diners can view the Atlantic Ocean across Beach Drive. Doug "D" Letterman, Eddie Jurewicz, Paul Mathis, Bill Noe, Bernie Bischoff, and Jim Colubiale were joined this week for some waffles and wisdom by a new member of the retirement circle and a former LCMR principal, Jim O'Neil, who was vacationing in Cape May for the week. After the group was escorted to their table inside the main dining room and settled into their seats, Jim O'Neil asked Jimmy C why a seat was left open between them at the table, and Jimmy C told him that the place was for Dave. O'Neil then wanted to know if Dave was going to be as late for breakfast as he was to school all those years ago. Unwittingly, Jim O'Neil had supplied the group with its Spirit of Dave Smith Story of the Week. Although the seat remained empty throughout breakfast, we continually told the waitress that we were waiting for another guest.

Aleathea's breakfast menu offers all the required egg, omelet, and pancake dishes as well as specials like Eggs Benedict and various quiches. Several of the group had omelets, and they were very fluffy and moist, served with home fries and toast. Our waitress, an LCMR alumnus, recognized most of us from her years at Lower and kept the coffee coming throughout the meal. When we even gave her one of our 'Breakfast with Dave' business cards, she wanted to know which one of us was Dave, and we all just simultaneously stared at the empty chair and said, "Dave's not here!" So, we explained the saga of summertime Dave and his Iron Man lifeguard heroics, and that he will rejoin us in the fall once he gets the sand out of his system.

Once our server whisked our orders off to the kitchen and we had another round of coffee and tea, Jim O'Neil mentioned that his daughter is attending Tulane University in New Orleans. When Eddie J heard this, he suggested that Jim tell his daughter to go to Preservation Hall and listen to the Preservation Hall Jazz Band, which Eddie brought to LCMR before Jim was principal at the school. When Eddie himself went to New Orleans, he visited the Hall and re-introduced himself to the wife of one of the deceased members of the original band. When Eddie mentioned he was from Mt. Carmel Pennsylvania, which is where she and her late husband originated, her eyes lit up. She explained how the Preservation Hall Jazz Band did the soundtrack for Woody Allen's *Sleeper* and that if Eddie was ever in New York, he should go to the bar in Manhattan where Woody Allen plays Dixieland clarinet on Thursday nights and mention her name and meet Woody Allen personally. When Eddie said that he did not know what he would say to a man like Woody Allen, Jimmy C noted Eddie should walk up to him and say, "These Pretzels are making me thirsty!" And so, we had our *Seinfeld* allusion for the week.

As our server placed our food on the table, the waitress hinted that if Dave should show up, she could easily rush his order through. Jim responded, "Dave? No, Dave's not here!"

Once we began to eat, Jim O'Neil looked around the table and recognized that everyone around him was retired, like he is now. So, he started to ask each of us how long we have been retired and found that Doug is now ten years into retirement, but Bernie is now 15 years removed from the classroom! Jim O'Neil then realized that the NJ pension system is so screwed-up because Bernie has been draining it for quite some time. Henceforth and from this day forward, the group will now refer to him as "Bernie 'The Drain' Bischoff". Then, Paul asked Jim O when did he realize that "he was not in Kansas anymore" in regard to his term as principal at the Erma School of Hard Knocks. Jim then launched into the story of the cat cadavers. The AP Biology teacher at the time requested that he purchase the dead cats for the students to have the same AP experience others in the state share through participation in this course. So, principal Jim agreed and requested the purchase of the cat cadavers and thought nothing more of the whole deal. These cadavers were something that the teacher needed to teach the class, and that was that. Then, when he arrives at the monthly board meeting, people from PETA are there loaded for bear (no pun intended) about the purchasing of these dead cats. That particular board meeting was an excellent example of why providing meaningful instruction to high school students is so difficult to do.

While we sipped on an after-breakfast coffee and tea, Jim O'Neil told the group of two separate trips he took. As a gift, the teachers and staff of his Chatham school district gave Jim and his wife an all-expense paid trip to Ireland! During the week's vacation, he managed to visit cities like Dublin and Cork along with many places in-between. We are happy to report that Jim did manage to tour the Guinness brewery while there as well. The other trip that Jim O was excited to tell us about was his trip to Taiwan. However, this trip was for business rather than pleasure. Jim, along with his Chatham high school principal, went to Taiwan to study how to introduce and offer Chinese to his Chatham school system. The community's response was so overwhelming that he needed to hire several more people to keep pace with the program's demand. At least the graduates of Chatham will be able to speak the new American Language if we ever default on our debt to China. However, Paul was not that worried because he feels that we have China over a barrel. Paul has discovered that China buys most, if not all, of its chopsticks from Georgia because we have the best wood to make them. So, if the Chinese look closely while they eat, they will see "Made in the USA" on their eating utensils. At least the USA has that going for it.

Once the bill arrived, Doug did his thing and figured that each of us owed $11.00 for this week's feast, which included a decent tip for our server. The food was delicious, the atmosphere was elegant and refreshing, and the service was attentive and timely. These attributes created a very comfortable backdrop for sharing memories and good times, which is what 'Breakfast with Dave' is all about.

SEMPER FI

8/16/2011

Cape May, NJ: On this mainly sunny yet mild August Thursday morning, 'Breakfast with Dave' returned to McGlade's on the Beach along the promenade in Historic Cape May, New Jersey to honor our friend and colleague, Gene Sole, who finally succumbed to cancer just last week. A record-tying 12 celebrants gathered together in Gene's honor including: Lynn Massimiano (our birthday girl), Paul Mathis, Bernie Bischoff, Bill Noe, Bill Carr, Eddie Jurewicz, Lisa Jurewicz, Doug "D" Letterman, Sue Crossan, Jim Colubiale, John Wilsey, and a special guest appearance by the American Iron Man himself, Dave Smith!

Also in attendance this Thursday morning was Gene's bottle of Wild Turkey (Rare Breed). Paul, Jim, and Sean Murphy purchased this bottle for Gene when the United States Marine Corp deployed him to Iraq while he was the assistant principal of Lower Cape May Regional High School. In true military fashion, he only accepted the bottle under the condition that they would all drink from it with him once he returned from his deployment. Upon his return, the one time all parties were present together, the bottle was AWOL. And so before they could gather together again, Gene became ill. Just this past spring, Gene came to a 'Breakfast with Dave' soiree and returned the unopened bottle to the group. This morning after breakfast, we will honor his memory by toasting him from this bottle, which stood at attention on the East end of the table throughout the meal.

McGlade's, which is currently celebrating its 30th season in Cape May, features all types and kinds of omelets as well as right-on-the-beach front dining. The menu also offers generous portions of pancakes, waffles, and French toast. All eggs come with home fries and fruit garnish while the coffee is not only fresh but bottomless as well.

Once the group was settled, and our orders were sent off to the kitchen, we all focused on any one of numerous conversations that spiraled out around the table. At the west end of the table, Lisa J made her intentions clear once again that this will be her last 180 days at the Erma School of Hard Knocks. Meanwhile, Sue, who also has the numbers for an early retirement like the others at the table, stressed that she will push on at the school for yet another year, maybe holding out on retirement until social security kicks in.

John then changed the conversation topic to how crazy Cape May becomes during these dog days of summer. He told of how he just recently went to the local Wawa in Cape May and watched a woman driver leaving the parking lot "T" a bicyclist crossing in front of her, driving the bike and the rider nearly 5 feet from the impact! While everyone ran to the aid of the bicyclist, the driver drove off, but not before several witnesses, including John, noticed the license plate number. Later that same day, John was heading out of West Cape May over the West Cape May Bridge when a car, waiting at a stop sign at the base of the bridge, bolted out in front of him. John immediately recognized the vehicle and the license plate number as the Wawa hit-and-run vehicle. When Jim asked John if he turned the number over to the local police, John directly responded that he didn't need to. Since John has her license number, he knows where she lives. And John left it at that. Sometimes we feel John is part Sicilian.

Once the food arrived, and our server refilled our coffee and teacups, Bill Noe brought up the fact that Stephen Hawking has recently denied the existence of an afterlife. Paul then asked Bill if this bothered him which led to our *Seinfeld* reference for the morning, alluding to the episode where Jerry, Elaine, George and Kramer can't find their car in a New Jersey Mall parking lot. George becomes frustrated that the group can't find the car and mentions that it doesn't matter, we will all be dead eventually anyway. Kramer asks him if that bothers him, and George insists that it does. When George asks Kramer if this bothers him, Kramer responds, "Not at all." George then reprimands Kramer by saying that Kramer's answer bothers him more than dying because its people like Kramer who will live to be 120 because he is not bothered by the notion. So, George asks him, "How could it not bother you?" Kramer responds, "Well, I once saw this thing on TV with people who were terminally ill. Every one of them believed that the secret of life is to live every moment." George can only respond by saying, "Yea, I've heard that; meanwhile, I'm here with you in a parking garage in Jersey!" We are all sure that Gene would agree; however, we are all still stuck in Jersey, but now without Gene's friendship and camaraderie.

After everyone finished breakfast and Doug "The Calculator" determined that we each owed $12.00 for this week's bill of fare, Paul, the designated bartender, opened the Wild

Turkey and poured everyone a shot. The group then stood together, raised their glasses and simply said, "To Gene," right in the middle of a bustling breakfast dining area. Then, Paul refilled the glasses, and from our seats, we toasted ourselves, 'Breakfast with Dave', for getting together and hopefully staying together in loyalty to Gene's legacy. The group then adjourned to the beach where Paul poured a shot of Wild Turkey into the ocean for Gene. On the way to the beach, Bill asked Jim about the more personal side of Gene because most of his dealings with Gene were on a professional level. So Jim told Bill a story about a colleague at LCMR, John Merrill, a now-retired history teacher at the school, who had Indian artifacts along with bones and a dear skull, which he prized above all, in his room. Well, early one morning, Gene, who was then the assistant principal, let himself into John's room, kidnapped the skull, and held it for ransom. Every day he left anonymous notes on John's desk or in his school mailbox in the mornings explaining the terms for release of the skull. John never really knew who was doing this either. So to keep him off balance, Gene planned to have the manager of the Health Club he attended give the skull back to him when he came in for his next workout. However, Gene never figured that the club enrolled two John Merrill's, and the manager gave it to the wrong one. Then, Jim said the story rings of an "IT'S NOT A SMALL WORLD; IT'S A BIG CAPE MAY" tale because that next day he came over to see his mom and dad in Wildwood Crest and his parent's next door neighbor came over to him with this box asking Jim, "You work at Lower Cape May don't you? Well, could you explain this?" When he opened the box, the skull was seated atop a nest of straw. This man standing before Jim was the "other" John Merrill; Jim thought he had just entered into the Twilight Zone! So Jim proceeded to explain the whole prank to him (in four-part harmony) and assured him that he would make sure the intended John Merrill has his skull back. In loyalty to Gene, Jim never told the real John Merrill who kidnapped his skull, and even to this day, he remains friends with the other John Merrill.

By the time Jim finished telling all this to Bill, the group had adjourned to the high water line on the beach where Paul had poured a shot of Wild Turkey into the ocean for Gene.

Semper Fidelis

GOODNIGHT IRENE!

9/1/2011

West Cape May, NJ: For this very 1st September Thursday, the 'Breakfast with Dave' moveable feast and morning soiree returned to the Bella Vida Garden Cafe on Broadway in West Cape May for some post-hurricane food and fun. Again, Dave could not attend, but he is now only weeks away from shedding his Iron Man Lifeguard superhero alias and rejoining us once again. So, this week Bernie Bischoff, Bill Noe, Bill Carr, Paul Mathis, Eddie Jurewicz, Lynn Massimiano, Doug "D" Letterman and Jim Colubiale all gathered to share some eggs, omelets, and memories, without Dave. Bella Vida's menu has a quite extensive and impressive listing of omelets as well as a variety of 'special' offerings like the Big Kahuna (2 eggs, 2 pancakes, bacon, sausage, home fries and juice or coffee) for $9.95 or the Little Kahuna (2 eggs, 2 pancakes filled with sausage, bacon, home fries and juice or coffee) for $7.95. However, one of the most appealing features of Bella Vita is that they offer some of the best grits in South Jersey and serve Costa Rican coffee as well. The Spirit of Dave Smith Story of the week is actually another dream that Jim had of Iron Man Dave surfing the aftermath waves of Hurricane Irene with Elvis. In the dream, Iron Man Dave and Elvis are paddling back out in-between sets, and Elvis compliments Dave on how well he could still paddle even with that massive iron man suit hanging all over him. Just then, a set of waves loomed ahead of them. Elvis made it over, but I. M. Dave thought he could just punch himself through the wall. However, he misjudged. The front of his board broke through the lip allowing Iron Man Dave to make actual eye contact with Elvis on the other side with just enough time to say, "Thank you, thank you very much!" before he was 'cowboyed' (i.e., sucked over the falls). Throughout the session, Elvis' hair never got wet! Once our waitress, Amanda, took our orders off to the kitchen and the coffee started to kick in, the conversation began in earnest with Bill Carr reminiscing about one of the very early principals of the high school, Melvin Boubolis and a fishing trip he went on with him. One December day, Boubolis took Bill Carr and Jack Conner, a Special Ed. Teacher at the time, on a fishing trip for Cod. According to Bill Carr, Melvin made these incredible rum-based mixed drinks that were quite potent and kept them coming throughout the journey in an effort "to keep everyone warm." On the way in, Bill and Jack were seated at the stern when the boat turned into the Bree-Zee-Lee boat yard and failed to throttle back. Bill raced up to the bridge to find Boubolis at the helm out cold from the booze, and so Bill quickly throttled back just in time to avoid launching the boat up onto Ocean Drive! Then both Bill Carr and Bernie started remembering how Boubolis observed them back then by commenting they either needed new classroom shades or that the shades they had should be kept even through the school day, never really saying anything about the lesson itself. Bill Noe also mentioned a time when Dr. Allen, an LCMR principal from the 90's who had minimal science background at all, once asked for a textbook so he could understand the Marine science lesson he just witnessed in Bill's classroom. Bill said Dr. Allen really needed a Marine biologist to help him know what was going on in the lesson. This was the group's Seinfeld reference for the morning, alluding to the episode where George pretends to be a Marine Biologist who is called out into the surf to save a whale. This triggered Jim to remember a time when Bill Stonis, an assistant principal, was sent to observe Karl Toft, a Marine Biology teacher. However, just next door to Karl was Frank Toth, a mechanical drawing teacher. Well, Stonis sat through an entire Frank Toth class and then called Frank into his office to say that the lesson was very well planned and delivered, but he would like Frank to explain how the lesson related to Marine Biology. Frank couldn't explain that, but he did explain how Stonis just managed to observe the wrong teacher. We were so focused on these stories that we almost failed to realize that our meals had been set down in front of us. As we cut into our own breakfasts, Paul picked up the conversation about lesson plans by explaining to the group how our deceased dear friend and colleague Jimmy Mullen wrote his plans. Paul said that Jimmy would write them as a flowchart from the top to the bottom of the page. At certain junctures of the chart, Jimmy would place a little smiley face sticker. When Paul asked him one day what the smiley face stickers meant, Jimmy told him they were there to remind him that he should tell a joke at that time. This little anecdote opened the "Jimmy-Mullen-story floodgates" as Bill Carr brought up the time he and Jimmy were going to LaSalle College, and Jimmy didn't show up for his first 8AM college class. Bill found him in an Olney Tavern, belly up to the bar with a beer and shot in front of him. Bill said that Jimmy had a ritual of how he would drink the two. First, he would sip a bit of the shot, then pour the rest into the beer and finally down the beer. Only then would Jimmy be ready for his first class. Paul then reminded everyone that yesterday was the first day back to school for teachers and staff at the high school. He also pointed out that a picture of the 'Breakfast with Dave' group at the Tuckahoe Diner was sandwiched between a picture of a cafeteria lady and a bus driver during a morning video presentation entitled, "Why Teaching at LCMR Is So Great." Jimmy C could not help but share another Jimmy Mullen story about the first day of every school year and how Mullen would introduce himself to his classes. Since Jimmy C taught next to him for nearly 25 years, he can still hear Mullen's opening day intro play out in his head, "My name is Mr. Mullen, and this class is 11th General English, or for some of you, English as a second language." We all agreed that no one had a faster or sharper cerebral wit than Jimmy Mullen; he was so extraordinary, which is why he is missed so very much. Once the breakfast plates were bused and more coffee and tea started pumping through our systems, the conversation swung around to how everyone managed through Hurricane Irene this past weekend. Of the 8 at the table, only 2 evacuated Cape May County, which actually bucked the trend of 98% evacuations for the County. Paul and his wife Landa booked a hotel suite in Marlton just off of Rt. 73 and hunkered down there for the duration. Eddie Jurewicz and his wife Lisa were in California where Eddie attended a wedding at a Malibu ranch and watched a full day of bands at a Ventura Music Festival organized by his son Chris. In addition, while at Amoeba Records in LA, he had the chance to meet Harry Shearer, who autographed a copy of The Big Uneasy for him and gave a review of the film in the voice of Principal Seymour Skinner from the Simpsons. Eddie said that everyone within earshot applauded his effort. The rest of the group stayed put, except for Jimmy C who had made plans to stay at a motel in Galloway until he discovered that even parts of Galloway were being evacuated. Also though the motel said they were still open, they could not tell if that would remain the case. So, Jim decided to move from Wildwood Crest and take his wife and Dad to his home in North Cape May to weather out the storm. When family started to question the sanity of such a decision, Jim's 89 year old Dad said to blame the decision on him because experiencing a hurricane first hand was on his bucket list. The bottom line was that Jim,

Deb and his Dad lost power at 6:30 PM on Saturday while power never went out at his Dad's Wildwood Crest home. In fact, the power was still out when they left for the Crest on Sunday afternoon. Well, if we are to believe that only 2% of all of Cape May County remained behind, then those "2%er's" are well represented within our group. Sometime during the conversation of Hurricanes and evacuations, the check arrived and Doug "The Calculator" Letterman quickly deciphered that we each owed $15.00 a piece for this week's 'Breakfast with Dave' morning feast. As always, the cost included a decent tip for our waitress, Amanda, who did a great job of putting up with our morning craziness. All in all, the Bella Vida Garden Cafe, once again, proved why it is one of 'Breakfast with Dave's' favorite places to share great food and fun times.

WAITING FOR THE SUN

10/6/2011

Stone Harbor, NJ: For this first fall October Thursday of the season, 'Breakfast with Dave' wanted to have one last alfresco meal before all the seasonal waterside eateries closed down for the winter or the temperatures just became too cold. So, the group decided to return to Polly's Place in Stone Harbor on 96th and 3rd where they were denied alfresco dinning just this past May by swarms of gnats (see 'Breakfast with Dave': "Polly wants a Prankster"). This time Paul Mathis, Ed Sherretta, Jim "J9er" Ridgeway, Eddie Jurewicz, Jim Colubiale and Dave Smith braved temperatures in the mid-fifties and ate alfresco out in the shade on Polly's back porch overlooking Stone Harbor's inlet docking area. Jackets and coats were required.

Once J9er realized we were serious about remaining outside in the chill to wait for Dave to arrive (Dave was out making a bus run and was about 30 min. late), he broke down and put on a jacket that he luckily had in the trunk of his car. So, while we waited for Dave, we had our first of several cups of coffee and studied the menu. Polly's offered the basic breakfast fare of eggs made any-which-way someone could want, really moist and puffy omelets that could be made from an extensive list of ingredients, as well as thick and fluffy pancakes. All the food was outstanding, and portions were sizable.

Dave finally arrived and argued to remain outside for breakfast, pointing out that we will warm up once the sun peaks over the building. The chef himself took our orders, and we settled in to wait for the sun. Since Dave had just returned from a bus run, J9er couldn't help but think back to all those fall sports bus ride adventures that he took while coaching at the Erma School of Hard Knocks. When J9er mentioned Dolly, the bus driver, who wore Dolly Parton wigs and had a few other Parton attributes to earn her nickname, Jimmy C had a story to share. He proceeded to recant a time the Track team was returning from the State Meet in South Plainfield, New Jersey late in the evening when Dolly nodded-off at the wheel and the mini-van veered off the Parkway waking everyone on the bus as the wheels went over the rumble bumps on the shoulder. Jim made sure to include her in the conversations the rest of the way home.

Dave's most memorable bus trip also involved the Track team, but this time Terry was the bus driver, and the team was returning from a weekend relay competition at Pinelands High School. Dave asked Terry if she needed directions or any help navigating back to the Parkway for the ride home and she declined. The next thing Dave knew, the bus was on a service road running parallel to the Parkway as Terry asked him: "How do I get over there? I want to get over there!" Jimmy C. offered a final story after Ed Sherretta mentioned how mostly all the bus drivers always felt they knew the shortest and fastest routes to anywhere in South Jersey. Jim agreed and told of a trip to Shawnee High School with Bob. This driver once took credit for discovering the Blue Route as a quicker course to Haverford College during Winter Track, when he made a wrong turn off of Route 206 and ended up on a dirt "alley" road behind some rural houses. Tom Mount, an assistant coach at the time, looked out the window and saw where they were. Mockingly, he asked Bob, "Hey Bob, is this the Brown Route?"

As our chef and waiter delivered our food, he told each of the omelet eaters that this was to be the best omelet they will ever have, and he wasn't kidding. The group began to tear into their meals, and the conversation turned to music and concerts as Ed Sherretta was reminiscing about how alluring Fleetwood Mac's Stevie Nicks looked on stage. In fact, Ed pointed out that at one particular Mac concert he attended, he was next to a girl who asked him if Nicks was a lesbian because she wanted to "make it with her." Upon hearing this comment, Paul immediately chimed in with, "Not that there's anything wrong with that!" This outburst provided the group with its Seinfeld reference of the morning, alluding to the episode where Jerry and George are mistakenly "outed" by an NYU Student reporter.

As the breakfast munched on, Dave began to place bits of food on the nearby railing in an attempt to entice some of the local bird population to have a little snack. All conversation then ceased as we quietly watched a few brave birds come right up and take the food off the rail. Not satisfied, Dave then tried to feed the birds by hand and had one take a morsel right from his fingers, prompting Jim to designate Dave as, "St. Smitty of Assisi". Dave then went on to confide in the group that once he found a dead Cooper Hawk in his backyard. However, when he called the Cape May Point Bird Sanctuary to come and remove the bird, they declined to say that they do not respond to calls for Cooper Hawks. So, after further investigating the bird's body, Dave discovered a band on the hawk's leg. So, he opened the band and wrote to the address found there, explaining the situation. Weeks later, he received a letter from the National Audubon Society naming him an honorary lifetime member for his thoughtful concern over the dead Cooper Hawk. J9er was impressed, for now, Dave is not only a member of the Cape May Shade Tree Commission but a National Audubon Member as well. Dave simply stated he was always thinking of branching out.

By this time, the first rays of the sun were finally embracing our back porch table with warm, open arms. At the same time, our chef and waiter poured yet another round of coffee and tea leaving the bill on the table in the process. Since Doug "The Calculator" was not in attendance this morning, Jim took the check, which was for 81.16 but was having trouble with calculating the tab without a calculator. He handed the duty over to Paul who had a cell phone calculator. However, when Jim handed the bill over, Paul read it upside down. Reading 91.18, he promptly figured that we each owed $20 for the morning's feast. Although the cost was a bit excessive, the group begrudgingly forked over their Jacksons. Thankfully, Paul thought this was a bit much himself, so he looked carefully at the bill again and discovered the problem before we paid the waiter with what would have been the tip of a lifetime.

After all the excess monies were returned to everyone, which was like an Abbott and Costello routine in itself ("I lent you three so here's a five and now you owe me two…"), the group sipped from their coffee and tea mugs. Then, Ed Sherretta, looking down at the water underneath the porch area, started thinking about all the change he would see under the water beneath the Fun House Pier in the olden days. This opened the door for Jim to tell of the time he had to sub for Bill Noe's Special Education Class and Karl Toft took him and his 4 students to the Bree-Zee-Lee docks on Ocean Drive to find sea life for Karl's saltwater tanks in his Oceanography classroom. Unfortunately for Jim, Bill's 4 students had no desire to hang out with Karl's students, and once they arrived at the dock, they started to disperse into to the maze of boats resting up on the grounds. Desperate to keep the 4 together and out of trouble, Jim attempted to tail them throughout the marina. While he was pursuing them along the dock area, he noticed a twenty-dollar bill in shallow water right near the bow of a moored outboard. Seizing this opportunity, he gathered the 4, showed them the twenty and challenged them to retrieve it without getting wet since they all had to return to school and class in about 20 minutes. Then, Jim sat back and watched as the smallest of the group was selected to take his shirt off, and then after asking permission to go out on the bow of the boat where the money was, the other three slowly lowered the lad, head first, into the April water to successfully recover the twenty. On the trip back to the school, while Karl was showing off all the interesting marine life that his class found during their trip, Noe's 4 students chimed in that they found a twenty dollar bill and proudly displayed it to everyone which garnered cheers and applause from the bus. From that day forward, Jimmy C was known in the Special Ed. Classes as "Mr. C, bill fisherman!"

With that tale, another 'Breakfast with Dave' was adjourned for another week. Polly's Place came through again with exceptional food and service, providing a beautiful backdrop for some great fun and laughs over another fantastic morning feast. And the birds enjoyed the show as well.

BREAKFAST WITH JOY BOY

10/13/2011

Cape May Court House, NJ: Clary's Country Corner Restaurant on 2 West Hereford Avenue and Route 9 in Cape May Court House was the setting for this week's 'Breakfast with Dave' morning feast and *Seinfeld* symposium. On this particular October fall morning, Bill Carr, Eddie Jurewicz, Ed Sherretta, Dave "Joy Boy" Smith, Doug "D" Letterman, Paul Mathis and Jim Colubiale gathered at a cozy center table to share some short stacks and tall tales.

Clary's menu offers all the breakfast standards from eggs to waffles and from pancakes to French toast. The menu features several daily specials including one that offers everything previously mentioned plus a choice of meat with coffee or tea. In addition, Clary's is the home of the original 2-2-2 breakfast special (2 eggs, 2 pancakes and 2 bacon stripes) for $2.22 (before 9 AM)! The coffee and tea was refreshing and kept plentiful by our attentive server.

As the waitress poured the first round of coffee and tea, someone asked for cream, so the waitress placed a cow-shaped milk container in front of Paul, Jim and Bill at their end of the table. They all stared at the cow head lid and then Paul and Jim looked at each other and simultaneously said, "The Pez Dispenser!" Therefore, the group had a very early *Seinfeld* reference alluding to the episode where Jerry places a Pez dispenser on Elaine's knee during a recital given by George's current girlfriend that caused Eileen to laugh uncontrollably and offend the pianist in the process.

Once our orders were taken and the coffee and tea began to kick in, the conversation focused in on Eddie J who was reacting to Paul's description of Pittsburgh's Sunday Steeler madness that he came across during his visit there this past weekend. Eddie J asked if anyone knew who Bill Mazeroski was. Most of the group knew him as the Pittsburgh Pirate second baseman who hit a dramatic 9th inning home run against the Yankees that won the Pirates the 1960 World Series Championship. Eddie J then told a story about how he went to his 5th grade class on the day of game 7 out in Mount Carmel, PA with a portable radio plugged into his ear, the wire running underneath his shirt and tie to conceal it from the Nuns. As he was doing his seatwork and listening to the 1960 World Series game #7, a Nun came from behind him and gave him an "I-know-what-you-are-doing" glance as she passed, but she did not call him on the carpet for the deed. Later, he discovered that the Nun who cut him that break was Bill Mazeroski's sister! If all that was not enough, Eddie J sat back and casually commented that today is the anniversary of that historic home run.

By the time we fully recovered from Eddie J's time trip, the server served our food and breakfast began. The conversation splintered off into two poles with Dave, Doug, Ed Sherretta and Bill Noe on north side and Jim, Paul, Bill Carr and Eddie J on the south. While Dave and company engaged in a conversation about Billy Garrison and a wrestling match against Vineland, Bill Carr offered his own Nun story. While he was working at the Saint Mary by-the- Sea Retreat House in Cape May Point one summer, Bill asked about a Nun he had in grade school who was living there then. Upon finally meeting her, Bill challenged her to name him. When the very old Nun drew a blank, Bill said that he would give her three names to guess who he was. The first name she gave was of a man who died in Korea.

The second was still living but incorrect. Then she looked directly at him and said, "Bill Carr". He told her he vividly rememberd the cat-o-nine tails she used to "discipline" her students. Obviously, Bill was a repeat offender.

As everyone slowly finished eating, the conversation focused on the north end for a while. Bill Noe, who just flew back from sailing a yacht down to Key West just so that the owner could sit on the boat, has decided that our country has turned into the "Have yachts and have-nots". Speaking of "have-nots," Dave is now again without a computer. His computer crashed for the second time in so many months last spring, but he never replaced it because he was using the computer at the Life Guard Headquarters on Grant St. However, the guardhouse closed at the end of September, so Dave resorted to using the computer at the LCMR's library. Recently, he went to use the library's computer and found that the library denied him access. When he questioned the staff about this, they told him that he lost a $52.00 book, and he now must pay the fine if he wishes to use the computer. When Dave made a remark suggesting he would not make the required restitution, Jim jumped up and in his best Mr. Bookman voice said, "I got a flash for ya joy boy!" This outburst gave the group their second *Seinfeld* reference of the morning, alluding to the show were Jerry is fined for a book that he took out in 1971 and never returned, and is harassed into paying the fine by a New York Public library cop named Mr. Bookman.

Speaking of paying up, the bill arrived and this time Doug "the Calculator" was present to render his services in establishing not only the individual cost for this week's feast and fun, which was $10 a person, but the actual overall cost as well. Last week, we could not establish the actual price because of the way the numbers where ordered on the check and no dollar sign was used (81 86). See, "Waiting for the Sun" (10/6/11). While we rehashed this with Doug, Ed Sherretta had to leave a bit early and missed the team picture. However, he did not miss out on another great 'Breakfast with Dave' soiree at a really down home and comfortable place like Clary's with fantastic food and great fun. In closing, 'Breakfast with Dave' would like to offer the following kernel of wisdom: When you walk outside on the street always wear a smile on your face, and you will be amazed at how many people will come up to you and say, "What the f#%k are you laughing at buddy?"

BREAKFAST WITH A SIDE OF TUN TAVERN

11/10/2011

Egg Harbor Township, NJ: On this second Thursday of November, 'Breakfast with Dave', or the oldest, established, permanent floating breakfast in South Jersey, ventured up the Stump-way to break bread at the Shore Diner on Tilton Road in Egg Harbor Township before adjourning to the Tun Tavern in Atlantic City to continue the tradition of celebrating another NJEA Teacher's Convention. On this mild November morning, Lisa Jurewicz, Eddie Jurewicz, Lynn Massimiano, Tammy McGarrigle, Paul Mathis, Ray McAlarnen, Jim Colubiale and Henry Weigel gathered to share some short stacks and tall tales. Unfortunately, Dave could not make the festivities for this week.

The Shore Diner's menu offered something for every breakfast appetite. From eggs made any which way and omelets made to order, to pancakes and French toast, the list covered all breakfast possibilities. For those who enjoy a little of everything, The shore Diner offered several specials that combined eggs, pancakes (or French toast) and breakfast meat of choice. The coffee was fresh and bottomless, and after the jolting little jaunt up the Stump-way, that first cup hit the spot!

The hostess seated the group at a long table for eight set up in an empty part of the diner, so they had an entire dining room all to themselves. The best comeback of the morning went to Tammy who said, "That's OK, I can imagine what I would like to have" in response to the waitress asking if she would like a menu. Welcome aboard Tammy!

After our orders were taken off to the kitchen, Lisa J, who is now down to 135 some odd days before she retires, proclaimed to the group that she was Ahab-like hell-bent on winning this year's "Brain Bowl" at LCMR. To that end, she painstakingly put together a "team" for the assault that will seal the deal for her, and she wanted Jim to be a part of this dream team as a community member. Teams are composed of students, faculty, staff, community members and selected "experts." Jim quickly pointed out that Paul would be much better suited for a competition like this since he is under contract from the Board of Education, he may qualify as a staff member. Lisa said she would look into that possibility, but she still wanted Jim on the team as a retirement gift for her. So, Jim agreed.

As our server delivered our food, the focus of the conversation around the table turned to the firing of Joe Paterno for not going "above and beyond the law" in dealing with his then assistant coach's handling of children (pun intended). This whole scenario reminded Jim of the finale of Seinfeld when Jerry, George, Elaine, and Kramer go to jail for violating the Good Samaritan Act. Thus, we had our first and somewhat disturbing, reference to Seinfeld for the morning.

Through the remainder of the morning meal, the conversation focused on a past LCMR superintendent, Ephram Keller, who more than likely hired all of those present except for Tammy, Lisa, and Lynn. Back in those days, the superintendent's office was inside the school building which probably made life a little miserable for whomever the principal might be, and this also meant that "the super" could be seen at any time walking the halls. Eddie J, who talked quite extensively with him after Irma McVey's funeral, reported to the group that Ephram is 94 years old and has just recovered from a stroke and is doing as well as could be expected. He then pointed out that Ephram's son, now working at Stanford, is a musical whiz who helped write a textbook that Colleges around the country still use in music history classes.

Sheepherding the conversation back to the past, Jim related a story about Keller told to him by Jack Connor, a then Special Ed teacher and Jim's running partner during the eighth period. Jack taught Special Ed in a D-wing room that was divided by a floor to ceiling bookcase to create two separate learning areas within his room. One day, Jack broke up a fight between two of his students and sent one of the combatants off to the half by the doorway while he remained in the back part of the room dealing with the other fighter. To his credit, the one boy went to the other side of the room and sat in a desk even though he was still fuming over the fight. Just at that moment, Keller walked by the open door and saw this student sitting at this desk seething and pounding his fists on the tabletop. Keller walked into the room and confronted the boy, reprimanding him by saying, "Son, where are your books?" The kid, still seething, looked up at him and answered, "Who the f-%k are you?" According to Jack, Keller's face began to glow in a brilliant hue of amber, and he left the room in a huff (or was it a minute and a huff?). Keller was not observed very much in the halls during school time after that episode.

After the dishes were cleared and we began to sip another round of coffee and tea, Henry wanted to know more about the annual gathering at the Tun Tavern during the NJEA Convention. Paul, who along with the late Jimmy Mullen, first started to make the yearly pilgrimage to Atlantic City many moons ago, told the story. In the beginning, just Mullen and Paul would travel up the Parkway to have breakfast, make a quick tour of the Convention and then belly up to a bar. Sometimes publishing companies like McGraw-Hill or Scott Foresman would have little parties in their hotel suites, which were open to teachers who used their textbooks. Jimmy Mullen and Paul would kill off the better part of the afternoon at these private soirees, not to mention some pretty good booze. When Jimmy Mullen passed away, Jimmy C came on board to keep Paul company to maintain the yearly tradition. Eventually, the State mandated that teachers must have 10 "professional" hours of in-services and classes at the convention. When the site moved to its new location off the boardwalk, Paul and Jim would make the trip to take two classes and visit the Tun Tavern across the street for a "shot of courage" between classes in honor of Jimmy Mullen. Then, one year Paul and Jim walked into a nearly empty Tun Tavern after their first class to have a drink. Diagonally across from them, but hidden behind the center of the bar, was Jim Ridgeway, a 'Breakfast with Dave' regular, and his wife Nancy, who had just arrived themselves for a drink or two. Without drawing any attention to themselves, Paul and Jim called the barmaid over and told her to set that couple up with another round. If they asked who bought it for them she was to simply answer "Jimmy Mullen". Well, she did what she was told, and Paul and Jim just sat back and watched. When the barmaid told Jim Ridgeway that Jimmy Mullen bought the drinks, his whole face became visibly pale, and he started looking around the bar to see who was there. Jimmy C even swears that for an instant he saw him shoot a glance heavenward. Mercifully, Paul and Jim made their presence known and J9er admitted that they got him good with that one. Then, J9er said, "Why don't we plan to come here every year at this time and have a drink for Jimmy Mullen." And so, we have done just that, and in the process Paul and Jim have shared some unbelievable adventures, like the "Waiting for Ridgeway" episode where Paul and Jim waited for Ridgeway to show up at the Tun Tavern and when he didn't, they went out on the convention floor and asked total strangers if they wouldn't mind if we videoed them asking, "Where's Ridgeway?". We were amazed at the number of people who played right along with us. And yet another time, Jim and his group couldn't find his van that he parked at Ceasar's because no one realized that the casino had more than one parking garage, and they didn't remember which one they entered. Misplacing the van was a real-life full-blown Seinfeld experience. Since they all knew the Seinfeld episode where Jerry, George, Elaine and Kramer spend the entire show looking for their car in a New Jersey parking garage, they were actually walking through the garage laughing out loud about the fact that this very thing was happening to them.

So, after paying the $13.00 a piece for this week's food and festivities, the group adjourned to the Tun Tavern to see what adventures awaited them there this year.

MEMORIES AND MEMOS

11/23/2011

Somers Point, NJ: On this mild but overcast November Wednesday, 'Breakfast with Dave', the oldest, established, permanent floating breakfast in South Jersey, made a road trip up the Garden State Stumpway to break bread at the Breakfast Shop at 910 Bay Avenue in Somers Point. Since a Thanksgiving breakfast was not possible, the group decided to gather on Wednesday for some pre- Thanksgiving omelets and anecdotes. In attendance for this last November 'Breakfast with Dave' were: Eddie Jurewicz, Bert Kern, Dave Smith, Ray McAlarnen, Paul Mathis and Jim Colubiale.

The Breakfast Shop, a favorite haunt for the locals who actually become mad in the summer when they have to wait for a table, is situated right on the water with the main dining area overlooking the Little Egg Harbor Inlet and the Rt. 52 cause way bridge. On this particular Wednesday, the locals were out in force causing the 'Breakfast with Dave' gang to sit at a table in a back dining area. The menu offers everything from omelets to pancakes as well as eggs done every-which-way a hungry breakfaster could want. The menu also had a few daily specials, like The Breakfast Shop Slam, which offered two eggs, two pancakes and two pieces of meat.

As the group began to sip on their first of several cups of coffee and tea, Paul unveiled his new "Martin" shirt. The unofficial 'Breakfast with Dave' T-shirt is a Martin Guitar shirt, which Eddie J supplied to mostly everyone in the group. Since Paul never received his, he went on the internet and bought his own version of a "Martin" shirt. Paul thought that since everyone was sporting a Martin Guitar shirt, he would be a bit different and wore a Martin Van Buren shirt, with "Martin" written on the front below a black and white graphic of the 8th president of the United States. This reference to Martin Van Buren led to the Seinfeld moment of the morning, alluding to the episode where George has a run-in with the "Van Buren Boys", a local New York City gang.

Once the breakfast orders were taken off to the kitchen, Eddie J started a conversation about what some well-known musicians did before they hit the big time. Eddie J said that his son Brett, who recently passed the bar exam and is now a lawyer, told him that while he was attending undergraduate school at the New School in New York, he would see the soon-to-be Lady Gaga handing out demo discs of her music on the streets around the campus on a regular basis. Then, Eddie J told of the time when he was a teenager driving with a friend, and they were stuck in traffic. On the roadside was a young man, just playing his guitar. Eddie and his friend decided to pull their car off the road and wait out the delay by joining in with the roadside musician. After some short introductions, the three began to play some blues. When the traffic cleared, Eddie J and his friend said goodbye to their newly found musician friend and went on their way. Months later when that roadside musician's first album hit the music stores, Eddie J discovered that he had jammed with Jim Croce!

Once the food arrived and more coffee and tea made its way through our veins, the conversation took several different turns. Jim asked Bert if he had caught any stripers this fishing season, and Bert proudly proclaimed that he just caught a 20 pounder near the Mulica River area just this past weekend. Then, Paul wanted to know if any of us had heard about what happened to the man who caught an 881 pound Bluefin Tuna. A New Bedford, Mass. fisherman caught this 881 pound Tuna in his nets. When the boat arrived at the dock, Federal agents are waiting to confiscate the fish. When the stunned fisherman inquired why such action needed to be taken, the Fed said that he did not catch the fish with a rod and reel and therefore, the fish was illegally caught. The poor fisherman showed the Fed his permit and license to catch Tuna, but the Fed just said that those permits imply the use of rod and reel and not nets to catch the said fish. Paul also pointed out that a 575 pound Bluefin Tuna sold for nearly $392,000. So, that fish could be worth half a million dollars! So, for now, the Feds have the fish on ice. This has all the earmarks of an X-File episode. The truth is out there!

Jim, then, pointed out that the Christmas shopping season will officially begin this (Black) Friday, and that everyone should start to consider what to get Dave for Christmas this year. Everyone at the table had experienced at least one of Dave's hilarious "Christmas list" memos, which were gift suggestions for the man who has everything–Dave. One year he placed a memo in everyone's box with the Vitruvian Man copied on it with following blurb beneath:

My dear colleagues,

Once again, in an attempt to ease the tension you obviously must feel each year at this most festive time (for each year you fail to find the perfect gift for me), I am supplying you with this handy guide. Perhaps you misplaced the one I gave to you in 1980. Bring this with you on those shopping excursions. As always, I enjoy many material things (refer to lists from 1981 to 2003).

MerryChristmas Happy

Hanukkah etc.

David
P.S. No frankincense!

Again, another year, he went on the PA and announced: "Please, no sweaters this year!"

So, Jim wants to put everyone on notice: 30 Shopping Days 'till Christmas! Stay tuned for 'Breakfast with Dave's' very own "Dave's Christmas Wish List". This discussion of Dave's Christmas list memos launched everyone into remembering their particular favorite, like the memo Jerry Guis, a science teacher at the school back in the day, distributed to "certain" staff members at the end of one school year. He carefully forged the principal's signature at the bottom of a sheet of legal high school stationary upon which he wrote the following memo:

"It has been brought to my attention that you are an asshole. Please take steps to rectify this situation immediately."

Paul's favorite memo was Jimmy Mullen's request for a class set of Thesauri for his room. The handwritten memo went something like this:

Fellow (teachers, colleagues, associates),

I (need, require, want) a (set, group, collection) of Thesauri. If you can (help, assist, aid) in this (plea, request, appeal), please have a (student, plebe, pupil) (lug, tote, fetch) them to Room 3B.

James R. Mullen
Primate of the Azores

By this point in the conversation, the group had not only finished their meals, but the dishes were bussed from the table as well, which only left the check for us to tally up. Since Doug "D" Calculator was absent, the deciphering duty fell upon his second, Paul, who rather quickly figured that each member owed $10.00, which was more than a reasonable fee for the good food and great fun we had at the Breakfast Shop. Once outside, a fellow diner who was walking to his car agreed to take a picture of the group standing around a shrine to St. Joseph the Worker, who everyone agreed should now be referred to as "the patron saint of the retired."

BREAKFAST WITH BLAKE

12/08/2011

Seaville, NJ: Grandpa told me he was taking me on an adventure this morning. He said we're going to Dino's for 'Breakfast with Dave', but it looked nothing like Fred and Wilma's cave in Bedrock; looked like a diner to me. Either way, the timing was perfect because I was getting a little hungry as we entered. Before we met the group, my Grandpa whispered to me that he hadn't told anyone about my coming to 'Breakfast with Dave' because he wanted it to be a surprise. So he carried me to the end of this big, long 'Breakfast with Dave' table in the middle of this enormous room with a whole lot of people sitting around it, and announces, "This, everyone, is Blake!" Then, he introduced me to each person beginning with the one person who was different from all the others, Janice. Next was Jim, who said he remembered me when I was half my size. Next to him was Doug. Next to Doug was Eddie J and at the end of that side of the table was another Jim, Jim Ridgeway or JR, who looked like he was already having a good time. Across from JR, was Bill Noe and next to him was Dave, the man himself, and I must be honest, I wasn't really that impressed. Next to him was Bert, but he didn't bring Ernie with him, and then, of course, Grandpa Mathis.

This man with a pad and pencil came with my own "special" chair which placed me right at the head of the table and right next to the person who looks so much different from the others.  I thanked him, but I don't think he heard me. As my Grandpa filled my bowl with Cheerios, the man with the pad and pencil took an order from each of the people at the table. Then, he poured this black stuff into their cups which they seemed to really enjoy. So, I asked my Grandpa for my juice, and I joined in on the drinking. I heard my Grandpa say to everyone, "I brought Blake with me this week because YOU HAVE TO SEE THE BABY!" Everyone began to laugh and talked about something called Seinfeld. I personally didn't think it was THAT funny. Funnier than that was Dave trying not to say anything I shouldn't hear. Meanwhile, I was so distracted by this Janice person (who smelled just as nice as she looked) that quite a few Cheerios never made it to my mouth. Through all the different sounds coming my way from the table, I made out the word "airplane" from the other end. I like airplanes. I wished for Santa to give me a book about them for Christmas this year. JR was telling a story about a man who owns and flies his own single-engine plane. How cool!? Unless, of course, the plane gets hit by a storm of dust forcing the pilot to climb higher than legally allowed to save his life. Then, Bert without Ernie mentioned something about a Dino's he visited while he was stationed in Germany. I wonder if that's where Fred and Wilma's cave is?

The man with the pad and pencil came back again with the food and the black stuff everyone wanted more of. Just the sight of all the eggs and omelets and pancakes made me want my chips, so I gave my pop-pop the "sign," and he filled my bowl with my second course. In between mouthfuls, I heard everyone laughing, and when I focused in, I saw they were all laughing at Dave. I couldn't understand what made him so funny? I'd much rather remain irresistible and flirt with Janice. As everyone ate their meals, Dave told everyone what I thought was a joke about two elderly married people. Dave said that an elderly married couple was having coffee together when the husband says to his wife, "If I should die first, I want you to take all my stuff and sell it." When the wife asks why, he answers, "Since I would hope that you would remarry, I don't want some asshole using any of my stuff." To which the wife replies, "Like I'm going to marry another asshole!" Everyone laughed, but I didn't get it. Why would anyone want to marry an asshole? Nothing any good comes out of there anyway.

My Grandpa couldn't help but match that joke with one of his own. He told of yet another elderly couple who were watching TV one night, and the husband asks his wife if she wants a milkshake. "Sure," she says, and the husband goes into the kitchen to prepare his concoction. While he's working, the wife yells to him, "Don't forget the extra chocolate syrup." "OK," he replies. "You could put some whipped cream on top," she adds. "I'm on it," he shouts from the kitchen. "Make sure you put a cherry on top as well," was her final request. About 20 minutes later, the husband brings her bacon and eggs. The wife looks at the bacon and eggs, looks back at the husband and said, "What? No toast?" Everyone seemed to like my Grandpa's story. Maybe that's why there were trays of toast still left all over the table.

After the man with the pad and pencil came yet again and removed all the empty dishes, he left a piece of paper with me that had all these letters and numbers all over it. Everybody thought it was really a scream, but I only had cheerios. And I brought them with me! Funny or not, I wasn't paying this. Besides, I'm a little short right now anyhow. You know, with the Holiday season and all that. So, I gave the bill to my Grandpa who in turn sent it to Doug, the group's official calculator. While Doug was doing his calculating thing, I called the man with the pad and pencil to come over to me so I could tell him my favorite butler joke, which goes something like this: "Jeeves, did you put fresh water in the fishbowl?" And Jeeves says, "Why? He didn't drink up what I gave him last night!"

While I was telling my story, Grandpa dressed me for the trip outside to the car and then home. As I was bundled up for the weather, I couldn't help but think, "So, this is what a 'Breakfast with Dave' is all about." Not bad. I guess I'll have to wait about 55 years to start my own or just hitch a ride with my Grandpa to the next one. But for now, God bless us, everyone!

By the way, only 17 more shopping days remain to get a present for Dave, and he really looks like he needs something special this year!

OBSERVATIONS FROM MEMORY

01/26/12

Wildwood, NJ: The oldest established, permanent, floating breakfast in South Jersey, otherwise known as 'Breakfast with Dave', brought its Thursday movable feast and morning soiree to the Key West Cafe at Andrews and Pacific Avenues in Wildwood by the Sea, New Jersey. On this rather windy January morning, Eddie Jurewicz, Doug "D" Letterman, Lynn Massimiano, Dave Smith, Jim Colubiale and Paul Mathis came together to share stuffed French toast with laughter filled stories on the side.

The Key West Cafe menu featured a daily $2.22 special of 2 eggs, 2 pancakes and 2 strips of bacon when ordered before 9:00 AM. The menu offered not only eggs and very delicious omelets, but on this particular Thursday, the special was stuffed French toast, which half of the group ordered and much enjoyed. Paul even had his French toast stuffed with blueberries. The coffee was fresh and flowed freely throughout the breakfast which was a tribute to the attentiveness and friendliness of the owners and staff.

Once everyone had settled into their first cup of coffee or tea and our orders were taken off to the kitchen, Paul talked about what happened the other day at rehearsal for his production of The Pajama Game, which will run at the Paul W. Schmidtchen Auditorium from March 15 through March 18. The cast was rehearsing a scene where one of the characters must "model" pajamas. After the young man burdened with the part stumbled through a few awkward attempts at "modeling" the nightwear, Paul discovered that the young man was a follower of Seinfeld (in syndication, of course, but a fan nonetheless). Once he knew this, Paul directed him to strike all the various poses that George Costanza used in the episode where Kramer runs a photo shoot for George in his apartment. As Jerry is walking to his apartment, he hears Kramer hollering out various directions and incentives to George on how and why to strike a particular pose, like singing out to him, "You are a lov-er b-oy. You are a lov-er b-oy." Not only did the group have a slightly early Seinfeld reference, but Paul is now seriously considering adding a sofa to the set and have the character play the scene like George. Even the high school play will give Seinfeld a nod this spring!

As everyone was enjoying another caffeine refill, Eddie J inquired if anyone watched the NFL playoffs this past weekend to see the Ravens' placekicker miss a last second chip shot of a field goal attempt to tie the game against the Patriots and send the teams into overtime. Eddie could not help but feel bad for the guy and wondered out loud how could he have missed such a routine kick. Jim pointed out that his miss was a result of not completing his usual warm-up routine before the kick. This particular kicker had various warm-up methods for each down he would be called upon to attempt a field goal. Off, away from the sideline, he was far from the coaching staff and relied on the scoreboard to let him know what down it was so he could warm up accordingly. However, the scoreboard had the wrong down listed, and the kicker was literally hustled off onto the field–cold. Jim said that he read about this very theory on Yahoo! just about a day ago. Paul even added that while he was watching the game, he wondered why the kicker ran out onto the field to make the attempt as opposed to just lightly jogging to his spot. So, the Patriots won, and we now have "Scoreboard-gate." Wasn't it the Patriots who were accused of stealing plays from the Eagles in <u>Super Bowl XXXIX</u>? Go, Giants! (and that's from some devote Eagle fans over here!!!!)

Once the food arrived, the conversation splintered. Paul wanted Eddie to explain why he paned a musician like Paul Schaffer as not worthy of the Rock and Roll Hall of Fame while Jim and Lynn were busy talking about their grandmas. Jim told a story about a time long ago and in a galaxy far, far away, when he had first met Debbie. He met his future bride-to-be while working at The Lodge Restaurant in Anglesea (North Wildwood) during the summer of '76. Back then, Jim lived with his grandmother in an attic apartment in Wildwood Crest over the summer months. Needless to say, Debbie came over quite a bit that summer and Jim's grandmother had a chance to get to know her, and vice versa. Then, in August, Hurricane Bob decided to pay the area a visit.

Since Debbie lived at the Mt. Vernon, which was an ancient rooming house in Wildwood, Jim thought she would be safer at his place, so he had her pack her bags and come over. At the height of the storm, where winds were clocked at the Wildwood Crest Police Station at 92 MPH, the northwest facing flat bay window in the living room began to flex. So, Jim started to duct tape the window to keep it from shattering. Meanwhile, his grandmother Pisano was yelling at him in pidgin English, screaming that he was ruining the window! Jim pointed out to her that if he doesn't "ruin" the window this way, she will not have a window left anyway; this made little difference to grandma. So, Jim, Debbie, and grandma sat in the candlelit living room watching the bay window breathe in and out. Then, Jim's grandmother stands up and announces that she will be going to bed. Before she leaves, she looks right at Debbie and asks her, "Where you sleep'a?" Jim explained that there is a hurricane outside, and he couldn't take Debbie home so she will have to sleep here with us tonight. To which Jim's grandmother responded, "I no like'a!"

Those were the days.

As the plates were bused and more coffee and tea poured all around, Dave offered the latest Tom Hank's Buddy Hackett joke from The David Letterman Show as a bit of dessert. He was extremely proud that he still remembered the joke which went something like this:

A Blind man's guide dog weaves its way through a busy intersection nearly killing its master in the process. A passerby who witnessed the crossing runs over to the blind man and asks if he was OK. The blind man, a bit surprised, says, "Why do you ask?" The passerby says that the dog had him weaving in and out of traffic, and a few times he was nearly hit by a car! Hearing this, the blind man thanked the passerby while he reached into his pocket for a doggie treat. The passerby could not refrain himself from reprimanding the blind man saying, "Wait a minute! This dog nearly had you killed, and you are planning to reward it?" The blind man says, "No, I just need to know where its head is so I can KICK IT IN THE ASS!" Well done Dave!

When the bill arrived, Doug did his magic and figured that we each owed $13.00 for this week's feast and festivities. 'Breakfast with Dave' had already spent several great breakfasts here at the Key West Cafe, including this past St. Patty's Day, and this morning was another wonderful "fast-breaking" experience. Good food and great fun make excellent companions at the Key West Cafe.

So, which one's Dave?

IT'S GROUNDHOG DAY!

02/02/2012

South Dennis, NJ: For this February Thursday, Groundhog Day 2012, 'Breakfast with Dave' selected the Southville Corner Restaurant at the intersection of South Dennisville Road and Route 47 as the setting for this week's moveable feast and morning soiree. Doug "D" Letterman, Eddie Jurewicz, Ed Sherretta, Bill Noe, John Wilsey, Paul Mathis, Dave Smith, and Jim Colubiale gathered to celebrate Punxsutawney Phil seeing his shadow earlier in the morning as well as share some tall tales and tater tots.

The Southville menu offered all the standard breakfast fares and then some. The menu included several different egg dishes as well as a whole list of various omelets, not to mention pancakes and waffles. Several daily breakfast specials were also offered including the Southville slam, featuring 2 eggs, 2 pancakes or 2 pieces of French toast, 2 slices of bacon or one sausage, toast and coffee all for $7.45. The coffee and tea were severed fresh and bottomless, and the waitress kept the group's mugs filled throughout the meal. Once everyone settled into the table in the center of the dining area, the waitress asked if the group was having some sort of reunion. Jim and Doug gave her a business card and explained what the waitress was about to experience was a weekly "reunion" called 'Breakfast with Dave'. Impressed that the group meets on such a regular basis and in such large numbers, the waitress carefully took the group's orders and refilled the coffee and tea for the first of many refills throughout the morning. The first topic of conversation was the subject of Groundhog Day. Phil had predicted 6 more weeks of winter earlier this morning, or in the case of the South Jersey area in general, everyone should be prepared for 6 more weeks of non-winter. Jim, then, told the story of how he, Paul and several other teachers had their own Groundhog Day celebration right before school began one Groundhog Day. First, Jim had to provide a little background on the event. Earlier that winter, in January, the area was under a winter storm watch for "plowable" snow. The event was to start in the wee small hours of the morning, but the forecast didn't hold true. By the time, the school buses were supposed to make their runs, the snow was still a no-show, but the skies were cloudy and the air cold enough to support snow. Annoyed that the snow did not come sooner to provide a "snow day," several teachers met in the main hallway faculty lounge to vent their frustrations.

Jerry, a science teacher, boldly predicted that the snow would begin falling by 10:30 AM and the forecasted intensity would earn the school an early dismissal. Jim returned to his classroom and kept a watchful eye out his window for the first of the flakes. At precisely 10:30 that morning the flakes started to fly and by 11:00 everything was covered.

After lunch was served to the students, the buses were called out, and school was dismissed for the day! Jim and company were so impressed with Jerry's forecasting abilities that they named him the school's official Groundhog meteorologist. So, before the opening bell for that Groundhog Day, Jim organized a "Groundhog Day Parade" through the hallways of the school, finishing at Jerry's classroom door. Jim, dressed in academic robes instead of a tux and sporting a top hat, rapped three times on Jerry's door with his yardstick cane. Jerry emerged a bit confused by all the people gathered in front of his room as well as the lights from the school newspaper photographers and morning announcement personnel, who all showed up to "cover" the event. Jerry saw his shadow and scampered back into his classroom. Later that morning, the announcements broadcasted that Jerry, the LCMR Groundhog weatherman, had seen his shadow and 6 more weeks of winter were in the offing.

Once the food arrived, Ed Sherretta and Dave remembered a time during a winter quite like the one we were in when they took a ski trip to an icy, snowless Pocono Mountain. Toward the end of the day, someone convinced Dave's wife, Anja, to make a run down the main mountain slope for the first time in her life. However, no one knew what she had made such a decision and began to worry about where she could be. Meanwhile, up at the top of the mountain, Anja was falling quite often and hard, soon realizing that she had made a big mistake tackling the mountain in such horrible conditions. So, she had the ski patrol sled her back down the mountain. When word was forwarded to Dave that the Ski Patrol had just brought Anja down from the slope and that she was not hurt, Dave thought that he would go and make one more run before going to check in on his wife. When Anja found out about Dave not coming immediately to see her, she was infuriated with him! Paul then interrupted Dave's story and reprimanded Dave saying, "So, you just had to get those Jujyfruits first, didn't you?", which became our *Seinfeld* reference for the morning, alluding to the episode where Elaine stops to buy some Jujyfruits instead of rushing immediately to his bedside when she found out that her boyfriend was sent there after an unfortunate accident. Then, with perfect timing, Eddie J tossed a pack of Juicy Fruit gum at Dave!

As everyone was finishing up their delicious breakfast meal, Eddie J asked Dave if the late Gene Sole gave Dave the Marine Corps hat he was sporting at breakfast this morning. Dave responded that Gene did not give him the cap, but he was a motivating factor in Dave's seeking out the hat in the first place. Dave then began to tell the story of how one day, years ago, he, Jim and Gene were coaching soccer together, Dave would always tease Gene about being a Marine. So, one day, Dave was driving a bus and wearing an Army hat which set Gene off, and he started in on Dave. So, later that week, Dave went to the Marine recruiter located in the ShopRite Mall on RT. 47 for the sole purpose of walking out of the office with a "Marine" hat. And that's precisely what he did, and he wears the hat to this day with great pride. Everyone wanted to know what the Marine recruiter must have thought about this middle-aged man coming in to talk about enlisting. But then again, it was Dave.

Once the dishes were bused and another round of coffee and tea made its way around the table, Dave offered his joke of the day. However, the joke proved to be a bit too off-color, so Paul came to the rescue with a golf joke: A foursome of guys was waiting at the men's tee while a foursome of ladies was hitting from the women's tee. The ladies were taking their time. When the final lady was ready to hit her ball, she hacked it about ten feet. Then she went over and whiffed it completely. Then she hacked it another ten feet and finally hacked it five more feet. She looked up at the patiently waiting men and said apologetically, "I guess all of those F*@king lessons I took over the winter didn't help." One of the men immediately responded, "Well, there you have it. You should have taken golf lessons instead!"

Just as Paul reached the punch line, the waitress left the bill for Doug, the calculator, to tabulate. This week's per person cost was only $11.00 which included a decent tip for the waitress who was very pleasant and did a great job of keeping up with the group's requests. The food here at the Southville Corner Restaurant was excellent, and the portions were quite filling. If Groundhog Day really turned out to be a Nietzschean "eternal reoccurrence of the Same" as depicted in Bill Murray's movie, then 'Breakfast with Dave' couldn't really do any better than be stuck in time at a place like The Southville Restaurant.

So, which one's Dave?

HAPPY BIRTHDAY, 'BREAKFAST WITH DAVE'!

02/09/2012

Ocean City, NJ: 'Breakfast with Dave', the oldest established permanent floating breakfast in South Jersey, celebrated its first anniversary as a blog by returning to the Varsity Inn at 605 East 8th Street, the site of the first 'Breakfast with Dave' blog a year ago. Gathered to celebrate the first anniversary and savor the Inn's great breakfast menu were Doug "D" Letterman, Dave Smith, Bert Kern, Ed Sherretta, Jim Colubiale, Paul Mathis, and Eddie Jurewicz. Except for Bert, all these participants were present one year ago when the suggestion was made to "get all this down on paper" Now, 52 blogs later, 'Breakfast with Dave' has returned to where the blogging all started.

The Varsity Inn menu offered an extensive selection of breakfast options from eggs made to order to hotcakes or French toast. Besides several three egg omelet specials, like the Jersey omelet or the Varsity Inn omelet, the menu offered several combination specials, featuring a mix of 2 eggs, 2 hotcakes or pieces of French toast, 2 strips of bacon and sausage for $6.95. The coffee and tea were fresh and bottomless and served in large mugs which suited the caffeine cravings of the group rather well.

Before the group even had their first cup of coffee or tea, Ed Sherretta wanted to tell a story about meeting Stan, a long time LCMR staffer, for dinner while recently vacationing in Florida. After the meal, both Ed and Stan used the men's room. At this point in the story, the waitress arrived to pour one of many rounds of coffee and tea into our mugs. To be discrete, Ed silently mouthed the punch line "Stan pissed all over his own leg," so that the waitress could not hear.

Once our orders were taken off to the kitchen and the group was alone again naturally, Dave had another "pissing" story for the group. Dave's story dealt with Larsen, another former employee, who told Dave that once, while in the army, he went out one night to the local town. While Lars was relieving himself from a night of drinking beer, his "stream" split-in-two, and he ended up pissing on the leg of the guy next to him at the urinal! The man then went on to beat the crap out of poor Lars!

Eddie J then startled everyone by stating that he played for the Cleveland Browns! At least that's what everyone thought they heard. Actually, he said that he played football with Henry Hynoski's father, who went on to play for the Cleveland Browns. Hynoski, a fullback, is a member of the 2012 World Champion New York Giants football team. Watching this year's Super Bowl was, therefore, something extraordinary for Eddie J. Ed Sherretta pointed out that he played high school football against Randy Beverly from Wildwood, and when Beverly became a New York Jet and played in Super Bowl III, Randy invited Ed and the whole gang from back then to the game! Ed still has the video to that game.

As the food was served, Dave told the group of his meeting Muhammad Ali who lived in a town close to Dave's Medford Lake's home. On a whim and without exactly knowing where Ali lived, Dave and some friends set out to find him. As luck would have it, they came upon a street where a large group was gathered outside a house and towering in the middle of the gathering was none other than "The Greatest" himself. Dave and his friends were so dumbfounded at finding him, that they did not get his autograph! But Ali did rough Dave up a bit.

Next, Dave told a story of Steve Riley having a pea-shooting fight on his college dorm floor. When Steve's adversary locked himself inside a room, Steve bent down to look under the sill. However, his foe already anticipated this and shot a pea right up Steve's nose! When Dave said that Steve had to go to a Doctor to have the pea removed and the doctor asked Steve how this happened, Jim provided the answered, "It was a one-in-a-million shot, Doc. One-in-a-million shot!", which gave the group the Seinfeld reference of the morning, alluding to the "AssMan" episode where Kramer ends up with a proctologist's license plates.

As everyone finished their meals, the conversation turned to how time sometimes goes too slowly. The conversation splintered into this direction as a result of Jim mentioning that this morning on his way to breakfast, he was caught behind a school bus causing him to be late in picking up Eddie J and subsequently for breakfast. Focusing on this subject of time, Paul even mentioned that he was always suspicious that Superintendent Keller played with the clocks at LCMR to make them run slower so the staff would work longer.

Jim then mentioned that during his last year, the clock in his room broke and because it was so old, replacing it took most of that year. So, Jim made up clock faces to cover the hole left by the removal of the old clock. For the first two months, one read, "Time will pass; will you?". From January to the reinstallation of the new clock by the spring '08, the other simply stated, "NOW." The first clock face actually made it into that year's EbbTide, the school's yearbook. Time always passed too slowly for the students.

As the dishes were bused from the table, the conversation remained on the past, recounting some of the more 'embarrassing' moments from the group's collective educational experiences. Ed Sherretta told of the time his wife, attempting to motivate a student to reach for a better career, asked him, "What do you intend to do? Mow lawns for the rest of your life?" when his father owned and operated a very successful landscaping business. Jim chimed in to insist that was nothing. One time, a new student was placed in his class. The only accommodation the student came with was to be seated up front. So, Jim did just that, placing the student in the last row, in the second seat just in front of the mounted TV in the corner of the room. A few days later, Jim was showing the class video about the Dust Bowl in conjunction with studying Steinbeck's *The Grapes of Wrath* and noticed that the new student had his head down. So, he carefully approached the boy and quietly asked him if there was a problem. The boy responded that he could not see the screen from his seat. Since he could have spit at the screen from where he sat, Jim asked, "What, are you blind?" To which the student replied, "Yes I am!" So much for reading IEPs.

Bert had an even a better moment from when he was the Vice-principal. He stopped an Asian exchange student wandering in the halls during class time and told him, "You'd better get to class, chop-chop!"

However, none of these events were as embarrassing as what might have happened next. As planned, the bottle of Wild Turkey was placed on the table so that the group could toast the first birthday of the 'Breakfast with Dave' blog. However, as the bottle stood on the table untouched, Paul, the group's designated bartender, discretely mentioned that Ocean City is a "dry" town.

Then, Ed Sherretta pointed out that two of Ocean City's finest had just sat down two tables away for a bit of breakfast. Needless to say, the bottle was carefully put out of sight, but what could have happened remained on the table as a topic of discussion.

Dave began by stating the obvious, "Well, that would have been great. We would have needed to title this week's blog," 'Breakfast with Dave' Goes to Jail! " Doug was quick to point out that Eddie J would have escaped the lockup because he would not have been drinking. So, Bert suggested that Eddie could have tried to raise the bail money on the outside. However, Ed Sherretta thought that if we had one phone call, we should have called Bill Garrison to see if he could have duplicated his magic spell and talk the judge out of giving the group any fines or jail time.

In the midst of all this entertainment, the waitress placed the check on the table, and Doug "The Calculator" figured that the individual cost for this 'Birthday Bash' at the Varsity Inn would be $13.00. Just like the first time the group came here, the food was still fantastic, and the service was as timely and courteous as ever. Some things never change, and the Varsity Inn will remain one of the better venues on the 'Breakfast with Dave' tour.

So, which one is Dave?

ITS: A CASE OF POSSESSION

02/16/2012

West Cape May, NJ: For this third February Thursday, 'Breakfast with Dave' brought (its, it's) movable morning feast and morning soiree to one of their favorite breakfast haunts, the Bella Vida Garden Cafe on Broadway in West Cape May. Joining the festivities for this week's gathering were Lynn Massimiano, Doug "D" Letterman, Eddie Jurewicz, Paul Mathis, Dave Smith, Ed Sherretta, Jim Colubiale, Bill Noe, and special guest AJ Colubiale, the administrator for the 'Breakfast with Dave' blog site. Acknowledging the 'Breakfast with Dave' blog on their website, Bella Vida offered free coffee to patrons who printed out the group picture at the end of each blog, brought it in, and correctly identified Dave. Flattered, yet mystified by this gesture Dave promptly compared his notoriety to Paris Hilton, who he said, "Has no skills to speak of, is good to look at, and yet still is a celebrity." The Bella Vida Garden Cafe's menu offered their usual outstanding array of omelets and daily breakfast specials, which for this particular morning included a Big Wave Breakfast Burrito that was a massive hit with several of the group. Another exciting special for the morning was a Surf and Turf omelet with lobster and crab meat as well as bacon and Canadian ham. Owner Chris Monge came over to say 'Hello' and announce that Bella Vida will now be expanding (its, it's) operational hours and be open for dinner as well. If their dinner entrees are of the same high caliber as their breakfasts, meals will be very successful this season and for seasons to come. Of course, a 'Breakfast with Dave' would be incomplete without Bella Vida's Costa Rican coffee, which our waitress Liz kept flowing freely throughout the meal. (Its, It's) our favorite coffee.

Lynn circulated a February '09 photo above from taken at Jim, Linda and Lynn's retirement party held at Congress Hall. Pictured with the group (rear left) was Irma McVey who passed away this past summer battling brain cancer. All those pictured retired from LCMR. As the everyone settled into their first of several cups of coffee and tea, Liz took the group's orders off to Chef Chris in the kitchen. Eddie J. talked about the Grammy's and Paul McCartney's jam with Joe Walsh, Bruce Springsteen and Foo-Fighters' Dave Grohl to Golden Slumbers, Carry That Weight and In the End, which are the final three cuts from the Abbey Road album. The only puzzling feature of the jam was how "lost" Springsteen looked when his turn came to take the lead. Also that night, The Beach Boys announced that they are planning a reunion tour for this summer. This time ALL the surviving members will be in the band. The Beach Boys are still a very sensitive topic for Eddie J since Mike Love tried to sue his son Chris over a comment that Chris made in a Ventura review of a Beach Boys concert. Since Mike Love was the only REAL Beach Boy performing that evening, Chris remarked at the end of his report that maybe the band should be called, The Beach Boy. Although the lawsuit never really materialized, poor Chris was put through the wringer trying to defend his comment. Dave took the edge off of the discussion by commenting that now that the group is back together, maybe their next surfing song should be titled, "Web-Surfing for Prostate Meds."

After the food arrived and everyone began eating, Jim referred to Dave's remark from last week about the Silver Alert signs that appeared on the Stumpway. Dave jokingly said that whenever a Silver Alert warning is posted, this means that Dave is out on the highways and byways driving a school bus! Well, Jim told the group that he was heading home from work on the Stumpway the other day and saw a Silver Alert warning posted. About a mile or so up the highway, Jim came around a bend and there, in front of him was a school bus! Of course, this was not Dave's bus, but the coincidence was just too funny not to mention. Then, Dave decided to tell of the "Bus incident affair," as the episode became known among the other drivers and the school's administrators. Smitty knew something was up. Too many faces were pressed against the rear bus windows. Behind the bus, a car was flashing (its, it's) lights for the bus to pull over. At the same time, Whistling Bill, another bus driver on the route, was CB-ing Dave to warn him that a car was chasing him and that he should be careful of stopping.

Nevertheless, Dave pulled the bus over, and the car's driver approached the bus door. When Dave opened the door, he was face-to-face with Todd Randle, who was not only an LCMR alum but a four-year varsity wrestler on Dave's team, which is another case of "(It's, Its) not a small world; (it's, its) a big Cape May!" Todd, who was quite disturbed, told Dave that one of the students on the bus threw a bottle out the back window that shattered his car's windshield. All this time, the students on the bus were yelling out the windows at Todd and generally giving the man a tough time. To his credit, Todd was holding back his anger, but he was slowly beginning to cave. Realizing this, Dave tried desperately to contact LCMR's head of transportation to report the incident, but Whistling Bill's constant warnings were tying up the channel. Finally, Dave managed to reach the Transportation Department head who told Dave to send Todd directly to him at the school to fill out the proper paperwork about the incident.

All this while, Dave was trying to keep the students quiet and not offend Todd any longer. After Todd left and Dave returned to the bus, he again demanded that the group on the bus calm themselves down. As Dave returned to his driver's seat, he distinctly heard someone say, "F# %k Mr. Smith!" under their breath. Dave immediately rose from his seat enraged, he yelled at the group, "F#%k Mr. Smith? F#%k Mr. Smith? Who said that?" Of course, no one admitted saying it, but the bottle thrower was caught after the bus security tape was reviewed by the administrators. Later, in the hallway, the late Gene Sole, who was the vice principal at the time, pulled Dave to the side to talk with him privately about the whole incident. Gene told Dave that when they pulled the tape, Dave is heard using the "F" word. Gene politely advised Dave that when you do such a thing, you lose the moral high ground. In other words, never fight with a skunk! Recounting this whole incident led Dave to remember Bill Cosby's "Why Is There Air?" recording where Cosby did this routine about a boy who threw a bullet into a campfire. When no one would admit throwing the round into the fire, the camp counselor said, "If you did that, then you do not have a good mother!" One boy then responded, "I didn't throw the bullet, and stop talking about my mother!"

Since the conversation turned to a discussion of old albums, Paul brought up the album, Another Monty Python Album, which was a 3 sided vinyl recording produced on two sides. Side two had both side two and three by using "Double Grooves." Paul discovered this while working at a radio station in College. So, depending on where a person would drop the needle, they would hear side 2 or 3. Dave admitted that back then in the 70's this would have been a great goof. While Dave was making this comment, he was pouring maple syrup into the remainder of his grits and stirring the mixture. Observing this, Paul asked if he was using a counterclockwise swirl, which became the first *Seinfeld* reference of the morning, alluding to the episode where Jerry discovers that Putty had stolen his patented sex move from him.

Once the dishes were bused from the table, the bottle of Wild Turkey made (its, it's) appearance for a belated birthday toast celebrating the first anniversary of the 'Breakfast with Dave' blog. This celebration needed to be postponed from last week because Ocean City is "dry town" and two of Ocean City's finest decided to have breakfast two tables away from our group. After the group toasted the future success of 'Breakfast with Dave', Dave spilled a creamer on the table, which was left un-wiped on the table throughout the breakfast to see if anyone could find Dave's face in the puddle. Then, Paul mentioned a cartoon that he had sent to most of the group about teachers "letting go" at a party playing "Pin the Apostrophe on the It's." Dave then mentioned that he always thought an apostrophe meant possession, but Paul stressed that this is only one aspect of the punctuation's purpose, pointing out that apostrophes also are used in contractions. To provide an example for Dave, Paul took the Wild Turkey bottle and used the little booklet hanging around the neck as an example. Paul said, "Look, Dave, if I say, 'The booklet belongs on its bottle', I show possession by using its, not it's, which is a contraction for 'it is'." While Paul was explaining all this, Dave was playing around with the booklet and inadvertently pulled the booklet off the bottle. Without missing a beat, Paul said, "Now, the booklet is not hanging on its bottle because it's now yours!" and the lesson was over.

While the impromptu grammar session was underway, Liz dropped off the check. Everyone had saved their receipt from their last visit and according to Bella Vida policy, showing a previous receipt reduces the current bill by 10% (Mondays through Fridays). So, Doug "The Calculator" figured that the cost per person for this week's feast and festivities was $13.00. Dave announced that he planned to pay his share in change and started to unload pockets of coins on the table, which gave the group (its, it's) second *Seinfeld* reference of the morning, alluding to the episode where Kramer tries to pay for some calzones with change.

And so ended yet another fabulous 'Breakfast with Dave' at the Bella Vida Garden Cafe. The food, as always, was outstanding, the service was terrific, and the laughter, memories, and camaraderie remain priceless!

So, which one is Dave?

Dave's suggested responses:

1. its 2. its 3. it's 4. its 5. it's 6. it's 7. its 8. Its

SILVER ALERT: Boomers Having Breakfast

02/23/20012

North Cape May, NJ: On this last Thursday of a leap year February, 'Breakfast with Dave' again brought its moveable feast and morning soiree to Uncle Bill's Pancake House on Bayshore Road in North Cape May. Gathered this week to share some flapjacks and jocularity were Ed Sherretta, Eddie Jurewicz, Paul Mathis, Dave Smith, Lynn Massimiano, Jim Colubiale, Mac McConnell with a special guest appearance by George Holden!

As the group slid into their seats at the long table arranged especially for them, Lynn found herself sitting next to Dave, who immediately said to Lynn, "Gee, You smell nice!" Lynn responded by simply saying, "Thanks, it's coconut." Sniffing the fragrance, Dave then said, "Ya know, that smells just like the beach!", which gave the group its first *Seinfeld* reference of the morning, alluding to the show where Kramer invents a perfume that smells like the beach.

Uncle Bill's menu offered a wide array of breakfast favorites from eggs to omelets to stuffed French toast, but by far the mainstay of the menu was the vast selection of pancakes that ranged from chocolate chip pancakes to banana pancakes, not to mention their great buckwheat pancakes. The menu also highlights several combination meals that include eggs, meat, and pancakes, like the Ferry Special. Also, most egg and meat dishes can be paired with an order of their moist, fluffy flapjacks by selecting the appropriately numbered breakfast from the place-mat menu. The coffee was fresh and hot, and Carol, the group's waitress, did a fantastic job of keeping up with the gang's caffeine cravings all breakfast long.

After Carol carefully took the group's orders off to the kitchen and poured a second round of coffee and tea, Dave began the morning's conversation by remarking that Paul looked a little tired. Paul admitted that his sleep last night was not "uninterrupted." Dave then mentioned that he too did not get to sleep until nearly 3 AM, claiming that he suffered from "Monkey Mind"; his mind just kept jumping from one distraction to another. Paul recommended Gene London's relaxation technique to help promote deep sleep. For 18 years, Gene London hosted the morning children's show, "Cartoon Corners General Store," which became a Philadelphia WCAU-TV institution from 1959 to 1977. Gene's technique involved concentrating on the part of the body, contracting that particular muscle then relaxing it and moving on to another part without moving the previous part again. This process is followed until the whole body is covered. Dave said that he knew of this technique and that he tried it, but it really doesn't work, to which Paul responded, "Are you calling Gene London a liar?"

When Ed Sherretta picked up on this line of conversation, he interjected that he tried hypnotism once to help control his eating habits. He said he remembered that while he sat there listening to the hypnotist tell him to close his eyes and relax, reciting the classic, "You are feeling sleepy" chant, all Ed could think about was, "This guy's full a shit!" Jim then mentioned an episode from *The Dick Van Dyke Show* where Rob became inadvertently hypnotized at a party, intercepting a hypnotic suggestion directed at Buddy which called for the victim to become rip-roaring drunk at the sound of a bell. Only the ringing of a second bell could sober the victim. This whole scenario was a perfect vehicle for Van Dyke's great slapstick talent.

Once the food arrived, Paul mentioned that he read somewhere on the internet that a man sold his comic book collection for slightly over 4 million dollars! Several of his original comics, like The Birth of Superman, went for at least 6 figures. When Jim asked Ed Sherretta what he did with his Willie Mays baseball card that he said he had, Ed answered that he put it, with many other now priceless cards, in the spokes of his bike! Jim admitted that he would "flip" his cards to win other cards from his South Philly friends, never ever considering saving or protecting them. If we only knew then what we know now!

However, Ed Sherretta still has the two ticket stubs, priced at $3.95 each, from The Beatles' concert at Atlantic City's Convention Hall back in the early 60's. These ticket stubs are reputably worth some money now. He also admitted that he could not hear any of the music because of the constant, incessant screaming of the crowd. Jim then said he had a real treat for Ed. Many years ago, Mac worked up in the casinos as a stagehand who offloaded and set up shows at various venues. One of his fellow workers at the time had access to tapes made from the soundboard from that night's performance at Convention Hall, and since Mac knew Jim loved the Beatles, he made Jim a copy of the tape on CD. So, Jim will now pass this piece of musical history onto Ed.

As the group finished their meals, Dave switched the conversation topic to the Western Channel on cable TV, where a few nights before, he had watched Rio Bravo and was very impressed with the cast. Dave then began to rattle off the names which sounded like Hollywood who's who. He said the film featured, John Wayne, Dean Martin, Ricky Nelson, Walter Brennan, Angie Dickinson….But before Dave could finish the list, Jim chimed in with "…and Yuk, the wonder Buffalo," harkening back to Johnny Carson's Art Fern and the Tea Time Movie skit that he did on a regular basis on The Tonight Show. This little ad lib triggered a flood of memories about "off-color" moments from the show that ranged from Ed Ames' tomahawk throwing demonstration to Dean Martin flicking his cigarette ashes into an unsuspecting George Gobel's coffee cup. However, everyone remembered when Zsa Zsa Gabor, who was a frequent visitor to Carson's guest couch, once came on the set with a cat on her lap. She asked Carson if he would like to pet her pussy, to which Carson quipped, "I'd love to, but you'll have to move that damn cat first!" Another time, Arnold Palmer's wife appeared on the show, and Johnny Carson asked her what she does to wish her husband good luck before a major golf tournament. Mrs. Palmer innocently answered that she simply kisses his balls. To which Carson replied, "I bet that stiffened his putter!"

As the last of the dishes were bused from the table and another round of coffee and tea pumped through the group's veins, the conversation switched to sports and the difference between sports like tennis and golf where everyone must remain silent and college basketball where anything goes while a player attempts a foul shot. Dave pointed out that an Alabama student, known as the "Face-man," positions himself behind the opposing basket and when anyone from the other team attempts a foul shot, he holds up a cardboard poster of him making an "ugly" face. Granted this might not be very loud, but the shooter may just die laughing after seeing his distorted fan glaring at him from behind the backboard. At that point of the conversation, George Holden, a retired math teacher and basketball coach from LCMR, who was the last coach to lead an LCMR basketball team to CAL championship back in the 80's, moseyed up to the table. He had been eating breakfast on the other side of the dining room and heard the group carrying on and decided to come over and join the fun.

As if to show off for George, Dave decided that everyone was ready for "Joke Time." First, Dave wanted to tell a hunting joke for Ed Sherretta: A 9-1-1 dispatcher received a panicky call from a hunter, "I've just come across a bloodstained body in the woods! It's a man, and I think he's dead! What should I do?" The dispatcher calmly replies, "It's going to be all right, sir. Just follow my instructions. The first thing is to put the phone down and make sure he's dead." There's a silence on the phone, followed by the sound of a shot. The man's voice returns, "Okay. Now, what do I do?"

Since that joke really didn't go over well, Dave came back with another: A man is driving a truck loaded with 20 penguins. A cop pulls the truck over and tells the driver that driving wild animals in a truck like that is illegal and that he should take the penguins to the zoo. The man agrees and avoids a ticket. The next day the cop spots the man driving the same truck still loaded with 20 penguins. So, the cop pulls the truck over again and says, "Didn't I tell you to take those penguins to the zoo?" "Yes, I did," said the man, "and today I'm taking them to the park!"

Jim, then, mentioned that tomorrow Paul will be a guest lecturer for his writing class at Stockton, and before Paul takes the stage, Jim shows the class a video of The Monkey Bar, where a chimp tells a joke about, what else, a penguin:

Customer Chimp: A penguin takes his car to the shop, and the mechanic says he needs an hour to check it out.

Bartender Chimp: What kind'a car?

Customer Chimp: What kind'a car? A damn penguin car, all right?!?!?! So, the penguin goes across the street to a 7-11 to kill some time and have ice cream. Penguins like ice cream.

Bartender Chimp: Really?

Customer Chimp: Sure. But because the penguin doesn't have hands, he gets the ice cream all over his face. **Bartender Chimp:** Is this goin' somewhere?

Customer Chimp: So he goes back to the mechanic, and the mechanic says it looks like you blew a seal. And the penguin says, "No, that's just a little ice cream."

At some point during "joke time," the waitress Carol, an LCMR graduate, left the check. Paul announced that the manager, Marty, another LCMR alum and son of the owner, gave the group a 15% discount which brought the individual cost per person to $12.00 for this week's food and frivolity. This group of boomers might sometimes forget where they are, but they will certainly always remember the great food, terrific service and fantastic fun that comes with breakfast at Uncle Bill's in North Cape May!

OK, so which one's Dave?

BREAKFAST WITH A SIDE OF LUNCH

03/01/2012

Somers Point, NJ: On this first day of March, 'Breakfast with Dave' trekked up the Stumpway to celebrate its morning feast and Thursday soiree at Fitzpatrick's Jewish Deli on Rt. 9 (New Road) in Somers Point, the furthest 'Breakfast with Dave' has traveled. In the spirit of the winter that wasn't, the temperature in Cape May at 8:15 AM was 62 very lamb-like degrees! However, 40 miles up the Stumpway, 'Breakfast with Dave' was greeted by a damp, drizzly 51 degrees. Go figure. Maybe this was the reason for Ray McAlarnen, Bill Carr, Bernie Bishoff, Doug "D" Letterman, et al., to fly the coop and head south for a few weeks or, in some cases, months. John Wilsey headed for Miami and the National Sailing Championships. To add to all the above, Eddie J called in sick and could not make breakfast this week. So, Bert Kern, Paul Mathis, Jim Colubiale and Dave Smith gathered to share some fantastic food and hash out some great fun.

Fitzpatrick's Jewish Deli's menu covered the entire gamut of possible breakfast offerings from bagels, lox and cream cheese to waffles and pancakes. The special for this particular morning was a very generous portion of corned-beef hash, which Paul, Bert, and Dave selected. The menu also offered a Hungry Man Special of 2 eggs, 2 pancakes, 2 sausages and 2 strips of bacon with toast and coffee, which suited Jim just fine! Another great feature of Fitzpatrick's Jewish Deli was the full-sized coffee mugs, which allowed the warm liquid to remain much longer. These mugs were kept filled continuously throughout the meal by the group's very attentive waitress, Joanne.

Usually, the Seinfeld reference for the morning originates from something said or done at the table during breakfast. However, while the group huddled outside the Deli's entrance, Dave mentioned that he had trouble sleeping the night before because his wife has the 'Jimmy-legs', which is what Kramer claims is the reason he can't sleep with his girlfriend. So, we actually had the first Seinfeld reference before we entered the Deli; this has only happened one other time (The Man, the Myth, the Legend). However, this morning, Fitzpatrick's Jewish Deli gave the group a first-of-its-kind *Seinfeld* reference. As the hostess seated the group, Paul asked everyone to be quiet and listen to the song playing over the PA, which was "The Time of Your Life," the song performed at the conclusion of the clip show celebrating the ending of the series. So, not only was this a great *Seinfeld* reference and the second in 10 minutes, but the song proved to be quite prophetic for this particular 'Breakfast with Dave' gathering. And all this before the group could put their first cup of coffee to their lips.

On her third visit to the table to take the group's orders, Joanne was finally able to send our requests off to the kitchen but not before pouring more coffee into each mug. Bert then wanted to know if anyone had watched the Academy Award show on Sunday night. Jim had watched the show for the first time in decades and was quite entertained. He mentioned that a reference was made to a "seat saver" in the audience and he felt that when the 'Breakfast with Dave' entourage reaches 10 or more attendees, maybe the group should consider having a seat saver so that the table will always appear full every time someone goes to the bathroom, which occurs quite often these days. This was yet another *Seinfeld* reference, the third so far, alluding to the show where Kramer was a seat saver at the Emmy Awards ceremonies and was inadvertently given an Emmy.

Bert, however, wanted to know if anyone had seen any of the best film nominations. The only one Jim saw was The Help, and he thought Octavia Spencer certainly deserved her Best Supporting Actress award. Bert said that he now wants to see The Artist after the film won the best picture and best actor. Dave added that he heard that not only is the film done in black and white but contains no dialogue. Paul then quickly pointed out that dialogue does exist in the film but is quite minimal. Paul also pointed out that even Mel Brooks' *Silent Movie* had one word in it which was "No," spoken by none other than the master of mime himself, Marcel Marceau, as he rejects Brooks' offer to be in the film. Dave then chimed in to admit that he always enjoys listening to the mime radio station.

The food arrived promptly and in such large portions – Oye! This breakfast would definitely take some time to process. Who else but Dave could have given the group this thought to distract them from devouring the food before them: "What's the difference between a bisque, chowder, and stew?" Paul immediately stopped Dave in mid- breath and presented, yet another, 'Breakfast with Dave' Grammar Lesson, "You mean 'Among' a bisque, a chowder, and a stew–not 'between'. 'Between' is only used for two items–for three or more use 'Among'". Dave stood corrected and was quick to admit that 'Breakfast with Dave' has taught him a lot about the English language; however, he still wanted to know the fundamental difference 'among' a bisque, a chowder, and a stew. So, when Joanne came around again for a coffee refill, Dave asked her if she could ask the chef if he could explain the difference to him. Joanne put the coffee pot down on the end of the table and looked puzzled at each of the group saying, "…and that's all you guys have on your minds today?"

Bert came to Dave's rescue by offering his own family analogy to explain the differences. "Simply put," Bert said, "A chowder is a son-of-a-bisque!" Dave still wanted to know how a stew fits into the group. So, Bert then amended the above with, "…and his little brother Stew!"

Bert and Paul could not finish the entire entree which maybe was the cause for the conversation to drift back to lunch duty back at the Erma School of Hard Knocks (a.k.a. LCMR) while the dishes were cleared, and Joanne poured another round of coffee into the mugs. Paul remembered a time he had cafeteria duty and observed a young girl who never once ate lunch for the entire school year! He and his partner who at the time was Janice Gallagher, a member of 'Breakfast with Dave', named the girl, Edith Not.

Bert's recollection included the late Gene Sole. During one lunch period, Bert observed a girl who did not eat at all but just stared into space. Bert then asked Gene, "What do you think she's thinking about?" Gene replied, as only Gene could, "Sharp things!" Now that the spirit of Gene was out on the table, Paul remembered the many times Gene would walk across the stage at this time of year (crunch time for the spring musical, which this year is *The Pajama Game* opening on March 15th at the Paul W. Schmidtchen theater at LCMR) and ask Paul, "Does this make my ass look big?"

After Paul figured that the individual bill for this great feast was only $9.00, including a well-deserved tip for Joanne, Bert told of a time his sister whacked him in the head with a cast iron skillet after he frisbeed a license plate that boomeranged back and unintentionally clipped his sister on the head. Dave then told of Dr. Betz who would make house calls to his Medford Lakes home and never charge his parents for a visit. However, on weekends, he doubled as the town sheriff and one Sunday he gave Dave's dad a ticket for speeding! Now that's Karma!

Before the group could leave, Paul had to pick up a half pound of chicken livers for Lynn, who also couldn't make breakfast this morning. While waiting for the order, the hostess informed the group that the owners had just bought a larger restaurant named JR's and that

Fitzpatrick's Jewish Deli would be moving within the next few months to a location just up the road. When that move takes place, 'Breakfast with Dave' will definitely be back to enjoy the delicious full portions of food, the fantastic service and the overall great atmosphere of Fitzpatrick's Jewish Deli again. The trek will undoubtedly be worth it!

So, which one is Dave?

PLANES, TRIPS AND SUNDRY TALES

03/29/2012

Erma, NJ: For this last Thursday in March, 'Breakfast with Dave', the oldest established permanent floating breakfast in South Jersey, puddle-jumped to the Fight Deck Diner in the Cape May County Airport for some food and fun over easy. With the visibility clear to the horizon, Ed Sherretta, Lynn Massimino, Eddie Jurewicz, Paul Mathis, Jim Colubiale and Dave Smith glided in for a morning flight breakfast overlooking vintage aircraft while in the proximity of true aviation history.

To dramatize how late Jim and Eddie have been coming to breakfast the past several weeks, Dave grew a beard while waiting for them to arrive this morning! Once inside, the waitress escorted the group to their window table just in time for taking off. After they were seated and fastened their seatbelts, a preflight cup of coffee and tea was provided while the group individually studied the menu to find what their own favorite inflight breakfast might be.

The Flight Deck menu offers all the essential elements for a great breakfast like eggs, omelets, pancakes, and waffles, as well as daily specials named after airplanes like the BiPlane which features 2 eggs, 2 pancakes and two strips of bacon. Even special orders are no problem for the Flight Deck chef who made Jim's Hungry Man Omelet Italian Frittata style. Coffee was hot and fresh and flowed freely throughout the breakfast flight.

After our orders were taken off to the galley, the conversation taxied by the following topics: The need to have a passport these days. The cost of Bruce Springsteen tickets. Thick as a Brick–II. Principal Skinner's (A.K.A. Harry Shearer) appearance on Conan. How the writers of Family Guy can "milk" a laugh (case in point, the promo for the show where Stewy naggingly keeps repeating "Mom" until the mother screams, "What?", and Stewy then sheepishly answers, "Hi"), and how no ensemble cast could match the original cast of Saturday Night Live, as well as Lynn's total contempt for Will Ferrell! Then, the group achieved lift-off when Ed Sherretta offered some Betty White humor, which went something like this: "Why tell a man to grow a set of balls to prove he's tough? You want tough? Grow a vagina; they take a pounding!" And with that, the group was airborne.

As the conversation reached cruising altitude, Paul reconvened the "Coffee Clutch Literature Circle" with a discussion of Bill Sterritt's play "Amortization of Smitty." After Paul assured Dave that the play was not about him nor was it about a mortgage, Paul summarized the plot as a coming of age type story, or "Bildungsroman," about a young man's romantic exploits.

Paul had even staged another Bill Sterritt play, SEPARATE CHECKS, on the Lower Cape May Stage some 30+ years ago. The plot was built around a restaurant where a waiter served three tables and how one table at a time the audience eavesdropped on the conversations. Other than the three separate scene structure, the pure brilliance of the story was how the waiter became the real vehicle of the drama, yet he was not physically involved in any of the tables' stories. This three-totally-separate-story structure brought Paul back to one of his favorite 60's sit-coms, 90 BRISTOL COURT, which NBC produced in a much similar fashion. Paul remembered watching the first of the 3 shows, which involved a Gidget-type character named Karen (played by Debbie Watson). Paul found her to be very stimulating. In fact, he remembered that "it moved." This statement gave the group its first *Seinfeld* reference of the morning (although the second time this one was used), alluding to the episode where George questions his manhood after a male masseuse "excites" him. Not that there's anything wrong with that!

Once the food arrived, and another round of coffee and tea flowed from pot to mug, Dave, in his never-ending quest to find snow during a snow-less east coast winter, announced that he was going north to Alaska! He will stay with his friend Jim, who attended a 'Breakfast with Dave' at McGlade's back in June '11, and assured Dave that Alaska has plenty of snow! Paul, who was the only one of the group to visit the 49th State, described the scenery as "breathtaking," which became the group's second *Seinfeld* reference, alluding to the episode where a doctor describes Elaine as "breathtaking" after describing a rather ugly looking baby the same way.

Paul kept the conversation engine humming along by asking if anyone at the table ever had the desire to buy back the last 10-12 hours of any day? Well, Paul stated quite clearly that he would pick last Friday, the first day of he and his wife's Orlando, Florida weekend visit to Anthony, his son, at Full Sail University. Before they even left town, they realized that they would have at least 5 1/2 hours of free time to fill before everyone could meet up with Anthony, so Paul suggested they go to Clearwater to a Grapefruit League game in the flesh. When Paul went online to seek out tickets, he not only secured two for the one o'clock game that Friday afternoon but discovered that the Phillies would be playing the Yankees, Landa's favorite team!

So, he bought the tickets. They both figured that they would arrive at the airport early enough to pick up a car rental, check-in at the hotel, then make the two-hour drive to Clearwater in time for the one o'clock game. However, when they arrived at the hotel, the receptionist told them that their reservations had been lost and that the hotel was booked for the weekend! (This was now the third *Seinfeld* reference of the morning, but Paul was on a roll, and no one wanted to interrupt him.) Landa stepped up to the plate and straightened out the mess before the episode ruined the plans for the rest of the day. They were now behind schedule but would still be able to arrive at the ballpark with more than adequate time to thoroughly enjoy the beautiful Florida weather and the majority of a good ballgame. However, the trip along Route 4 was constant stop-and-go-traffic for 2 hours; traffic would move at 70 mph for miles then suddenly stop dead for minutes! With the stadium looming ahead of them like some sort of grail (or golem, depending on your point of view), traffic again came to a dead stop from about 70 mph. Paul managed to stop the car and watched through his rearview mirror as a GMC Sierra bore down on him. Luckily, the man in the Sierra stopped just short of hitting Paul, but the school bus in back of the Sierra didn't and slammed into the rear of the truck which then crushed the rear end of Paul's vehicle rendering it un-drivable. Luckily, Tampa's airport was nearby and had the same rental agency, so three hours later the car was finally towed and Paul and Landa headed back to Orlando – the game was over, and worse, the Phillies lost!

Throughout Paul's saga, the dishes were quietly bused from the table, and another round of coffee and tea was poured. As the conversation prepared for its descent into another day at the shore, Ed Sherretta decided that a joke would take our minds off the impending reentry. So, we put our bodies in an upright position and listened to the story about Bubba, the redneck:

Bubba, the redneck, was barbecuing a venison steak on a Friday evening during Lent. Catholics, who lived all around him, were eating fish but were bothered a bit by the temptation. So, they talked to the local priest who agreed to speak with Bubba about converting and thus quit the Friday venison grilling. During their conversation, the priest did indeed talk Bubba into converting to Catholicism. Finally, the priest raised his hands over Bubba and said, "You were born a Methodist. You were raised a Methodist, but now you are a Catholic!" The priest then sent him on his way to follow his new found religion.

The next Friday, Bubba was out in the back again grilling a venison steak. The neighbors again called on the priest to confront Bubba about his actions. As the priest approached Bubba to speak with him, he saw Bubba raise his arms over the steak as if in benediction and heard him say, "You was born a deer. You was raised a deer, but now you is a catfish!"

Since the conversation was put in a brief holding pattern, Dave decided to add his own joke about an Italian funeral to help pass the spare moments:

An Italian man was leaving a convenience store with his espresso when he noticed a most unusual Italian funeral procession approaching the nearby cemetery. A black hearse was followed by a second black hearse about 50 feet behind the first one. Behind the second hearse was a solitary Italian man walking a dog on a leash. Behind him, a short distance back were about 200 men walking in single file.

The man couldn't stand the curiosity. He respectfully approached the Italian man walking the dog and began a conversation:

"I am so sorry for your loss. And this may be a bad time to disturb you, but I've never seen an Italian funeral like this. Whose funeral is it?"

"My wife's."

"What happened to her?"

"She yelled at me and my dog attacked and killed her."

He inquired further, "But who is in the second hearse?"

"My mother-in-law," the Italian man answered. "She was trying to help my wife when the dog turned on her."

A very poignant and touching moment of Italian brotherhood and silence passed between the two men before the one asked the other, "Can I borrow the dog?"

He looks behind him at those following and says, "Get in line." As the conversation finally made a smooth and soft touch down, Paul determined that the group's breakfast at the Flight Deck Diner would cost $11.00 per person, including a well-earned tip for our "flight attendant" who catered to the group's every whim, even taking the group photo. As an added feature, each of the group was given a frequent flyer card to earn a free breakfast! Even without this card, 'Breakfast with Dave' would fly this breakfast airline again and again.

So, which one's Dave?

"WELL, I READ IT IN THE PRESS"

04/05/12

West Cape May, NJ: For this Holy Thursday morning, 'Breakfast with Dave' made a pilgrimage back to its favorite gathering place, The Bella Vida Garden Cafe on Broadway in West Cape May. On this sunny and mild April morning, Ed Sherretta, Dave Smith, Bernie Bischoff, Wayne Mazurek, Jim Colubiale, Doug "D" Letterman, Nan LaCorte, Bill Noe, Eddie Jurewicz, Paul Mathis, Lynn Massimiano and John Wilsey gathered to break some toast and spread some Easter joy. This turnout now officially ties the record of 12 celebrants set at both Steve's 47 Cafe on Route 47 and this past Christmas at Hemingway's in Cape May. Ironically, the group was one member short of the required 13 and would not be able to re-create the Last Supper on Holy Thursday. Indeed, this week's group was so large that the Bella Vida even opened an antechamber dining area for the group to sit together at one large table, much like what had gone down over 2,000 years ago but a little later in the day.

Bella Vida's menu continues to offer outstanding breakfast entrees that are both creative and delicious as well as healthy! This week one of the favorite morning specials was the Sweet Potato Flap Jacks, which Lynn said were sinfully delicious. However, the real hit with nearly half of the group was the Breakfast Burrito. The Costa Rican Coffee was again in high demand and kept flowing throughout the meal by the attentive and very patient wait staff. A cacophony of conversations hovered above the table. No wonder four different apostles needed to write about the Last Supper!

But as the first waves of caffeine hit the bloodstream, the conversation locked onto Bernie telling of his encounter with a sick deer stalking one of the ski runs up in Vermont. After several other skiers reported seeing the deer wander aimlessly onto the ski path, the ski patrol decided that for the safety of the skiers and the deer, the animal needed to be put down, which Bernie was quick to acknowledge was very sad. Dave then mentioned that he always wanted to see an elk. One time he was brought to a valley where elk would gather at sunset. He actually thought he could feed the elk! At least he wasn't like W. C. Fields who would excuse himself in *The Fatal Glass of Bear* to "go and MILK the elk." Dave said the signs were posted all over warning not to put out any food whatsoever because this would most likely attract bears. Eddie Jurewicz remembered reading about a man somewhere who would welcome bears onto his property. From the other end of the table, Ed Sherretta added that unfortunately, the man was killed by one of those bears! This disclosure led to the story of Bernie and the Bear. One day, Bernie caught a bear eating the peanut butter out of his backyard bird feeder up in Vermont. Bernie tried several unsuccessful attempts (at various levels of aggression) to try to shoo-it-away, but buddy bear would have none of it.

Having eaten all the peanut butter, the bear left the bird feeder in favor of ransacking his garage. When the bear finally had enough to keep him going for the rest of the winter, he left without incident. When Bernie investigated the damage, he found bird feed everywhere from the many bags Bernie stored there for the local bird population to rely on for winter. Fortunately, for all of us, this winter was not severe at all. As part of the damage, Bernie found an iron rod that the bear had bent in his crazed attack on the bird feed storage cage. To this day, Bernie has yet to find anyone who can bend that bar back to its original position. He even tried having the bar torched to melt it back to shape, and even that didn't work. The group suggested that maybe Bernie should leave the bar in the garage and hope that super bear returns and bends the bar back for him.

After the experience of having 12 people talking at once while trying to order coffee, the group was gracious enough to use their "little" voices while everyone ordered their meal. The cone of silence that suddenly descended over the table was eerie, but it made the process of placing the orders run much more efficiently, not to mention quickly. Once the coffee and teacups were filled again, everyone welcomed John Wilsey back from his annual visit to Hawaii. John was more concerned about the shark attack two days ago just two miles from where he surfed most of the time he was on the North Shore. John also added that tourists are offered the chance to climb into shark cages and feed tiger sharks just off the North Shore Coast! That's stretching the aloha spirit just a bit too far everyone thought.

Wayne, who now lives 100 miles from the Canadian Border in a town called Glens-falls, went to a free folk concert at a local library. The duet, a man and a woman, were excellent Wayne said, and like most folk concerts, they performed a set where they wanted audience participation. Behind Wayne and his wife sat a woman who not only sang along but did so in near perfect alto harmony. At one point, Wayne said that even the folk singers themselves complimented the lady, who turned out to be a local opera diva who really liked this particular folk duo and followed them from gig to gig. Meanwhile, at the other end of the table, Ed Sherretta was explaining that a fecal transplant was a procedure for people who have a hard time breaking down food in their stomachs and needed some help to be regular. When Dave asked Ed where he had heard of this, Ed replied that he read it in The Press.

Once all the food arrived and each group member's meal sat before them in all its delicious glory, Wayne mentioned that he saw *Jersey Boys* at the theatre just recently and was impressed to discover all that went on in the background of the Four Seasons' career. Jim added that Frankie Valli's real name was Castelluccio, which sounded a lot like the name of the high school principal mostly everyone at the table worked for at the Erma School of Hard Knocks. Wayne then pointed out that while Frankie Valli and the Four Seasons played the old Wildwood clubs on Pacific Avenue back in the day, he had the opportunity to meet him. Jim also had a close encounter with the falsetto king when he was 16 and suffering from a severe sinus infection which closed his left eye and locked his jaw nearly shut, deforming his face into some elephant man- like creature. Jim was scheduled to have a procedure done at the office of Dr. Fury, an ears, nose and throat specialist located in Wildwood to eliminate the pressure building inside his head. Just before his treatment was to begin, the doctor asked Jim if he could wait a bit because an emergency just came into the office and he needed to take care of it. As Jim was leaving the treatment room, he came face-to-face with Frankie Valli who was coming in to have his throat sprayed for his shows that night. Jim said that he was so self-conscious of his appearance that he didn't want to have Frankie Valli look at him because he looked so hideous. This became the *Seinfeld* reference for the morning alluding to the episode where Kramer opens up his apartment for smoking, and when Jerry says that his face looks like an old catcher's mitt and that his teeth are all yellow, Kramer responds with, "Look away; I'm hideous!"

As everyone was finishing up their breakfast, Paul mentioned that plans are in the works for Rocky, the Musical! Yes, that's right, the Rock is coming back for another round! Wayne corrected a misconception that most people had about the original when he pointed out that Rocky Balboa was not modeled on Rocky Marciano but on the Bayonne Brawler, Chuck Wepner, who went 15 rounds with then World Champion Mohammad Ali in 1975. In the ninth round, Wepner knocked Ali down although Ali later would say that Wepner stepped on his foot. When Wepner went to his corner, he supposedly said to his manager, "Start the car. We are going to the bank. We are going to be millionaires!" To which Wepner's manager replied, "You better turn around. He's getting up and he looks pissed off!"

Noticing that everyone was finished their meal, Jim announced that the breakfast joke time had arrived. Jim prefaced his joke by saying that he could still hear the late Jimmy Mullen tell this joke:

A crusty old golfer comes in from a round of golf at a new course and heads into the grill room. As he passes through the swinging doors, he sees a sign hanging over the bar: COLD BEER: $2.00 HAMBURGER: $2.50 CHEESEBURGER: $2.50 CHICKEN SANDWICH: $3.50 HAND JOB: $50.00 Checking his wallet to be sure he had the necessary payment, the old golfer walks up to the bar and beckons to the exceptionally attractive female bartender who is serving drinks to a couple of sun-drenched golfers. She glides down the bar to the old golfer.

"Yes?" she inquires with a wide, knowing smile, "May I help you?"

The old golfer leans over the bar and whispers, "I was wondering, young lady, are you the one who gives the hand jobs?"

She looks into his eyes with that wide smile and purrs, "Yes sir, I sure am."

"The old golfer leans closer and says softly into her left ear, "Well, wash your hands really good because I want a cheeseburger."

At some point during joke time, the check was left for Doug, the Calculator, to figure out how much each of the group owed for this week's holiday feast. As Doug was doing his math thing at one end of the table, Ed Sherretta's cell phone was ringing at the other end. Ed announced that the call was from Jimmy "J9er" Ridgeway who was just checking in from poolside at a Hilton Head Hotel. Paul quickly pointed out that J9er was the group's 13th celebrant, stating, "That's our Judas!"

Doug figured that this week's banquet at Bella Vida came to $14.00 per person, but the fun and friendship shared at the table this Holy Thursday morning was the true measure of this 'Breakfast with Dave' get together and the best reflection of the Easter season. Have a Happy and joyous Easter!

So, which one's Dave?

THE RETURN OF THE TWELVE

04/12/2012

Cape May Court House, NJ: On this particularly windy but sunny and seasonably cool April Thursday, the 'Breakfast with Dave' entourage moseyed up Route 47 to Steve's Cafe 47 Diner for their weekly morning soiree and moveable feast. Again, record-tying numbers gathered to share some great times along with excellent food. Eddie Jurewicz, Ed Sherretta, Jim Colubiale, Bill Carr, Lynn Massimiano, Paul Mathis, Doug "D" Letterman, Bernie Bischoff, Capt. Bill Garrison, Bert Kern and special guests soon-to-be-retired Lisa Jurewicz and "Ed Norton" himself, Matt Sutter all came together this morning to share in the fun and food. Dave's absence did not go unnoticed. At first, the group thought that Dave had made good on his decision to go to Alaska for a few days to visit his buddy, Jim. But this proved to be only half right. Dave was all set to go, but at the last minute became sick and missed his flight. No worries though, because he took out flight insurance. Other notable absentees were John Wilsey who went to Hatteras for Easter Week and Bill Noe who had to deliver a boat to Florida.

Steve's Cafe 47 Diner offered a wide variety of breakfast ideas including made to order eggs to waffles with strawberries and whipped cream (shown here). The menu also offered several daily specials, including Jim's favorite, Pigs in a Blanket, which features an egg, bacon, and sausage all wrapped in their own pancake. The coffee and tea were all severed piping hot and freshly brewed.

After the first round of coffee and tea hit the table, the conversation splintered into three directions. At one end of the table, Lisa J, Eddie J, and Ed Sherretta were talking about the benefits of using a juicer as well as their mutual experiences in Europe. Eddie mentioned that next week he will be going to California and plans to go on a "Tom Waits Tour" which will take him to places where his favorite singer/songwriter lived and played in California. Jim wanted to know if he was going to ride on a yellow school bus and receive a complimentary bag lunch, which became the first *Seinfeld* reference of the morning, alluding to the episode where Kramer runs a "Peterman Reality Tour" through New York City. Meanwhile, in the middle of the table, Paul was updating Bill on his ill-fated attempt to see a Phillies game in Clearwater, while at the other end, Capt. Bill, Matt, and Bert were talking about how the spring fishing season is officially ramping up. Speaking of fishing, Bill Carr related a story that his son Chris, who is an avid surfer and excellent surfboard repair technician, told him of his last surf session at the rocks this past Tuesday. According to Bill Carr, his son Chris was gearing up and preparing to enter the water, when he saw Robbie "The Lord of the Rocks" Goodman take off on a wave. At that moment, a dolphin popped out of the same wave right next to him with a striper as big as a dog in its mouth! Chris said as all the surfers watched, the dolphin pod pinned up the school of striper bass against the rocks and then enjoyed a virtual fishing frenzy while the suffers were left alone to feast uninterruptedly on the waves.

After the group's order was taken off to the kitchen and another round of coffee and tea was poured, the conversation focused on the New Cape May Convention Hall, which will open this Memorial Day Weekend. Concerts at the new venue will be sponsored by Richard Stockton College of New Jersey. One of the first concerts will feature Gerry and the Pacemakers of "Ferry Across the Mersey" fame. Then the whole conversation steered right into the vast parking problem that already exists in Cape May. Eddie and Lisa J said that just this past weekend they went over to Cape May to buy a few Cape May sweatshirts for Eddie to take to California for his son Chris and his wife Amy, and they couldn't find a parking space! And this is only April! What will parking be like when the first concert takes to the stage in the summer? Even Jim had a Cape May parking horror story from the 80's when he came into town for a half-priced wet suit sale. He found a spot in the back of the mall with a few minutes left on the meter. Figuring that he was just going to run in, buy the suit and leave, Jim didn't pump any more quarters into the meter. When he returned to his car minutes later, he found a $35.00 parking ticket on his windshield, which destroyed the whole profit margin on the wet suit deal. Matt chimed in to say that the meter police were probably hiding and salivating while he was parking.

At this point, the food arrived, and after all twelve orders were carefully delivered and more coffee and tea was supplied, Ed Sherretta told of his $600.00 parking space. When he was operating a little restaurant on the promenade one summer, Tara, his daughter, went out one afternoon to feed the meter for the parking spot in front of the store where she had parked. No sooner did she return from putting more money in the meter, she noticed that a parking ticket was on the windshield and the meter was blinking red, which made Ed start seeing red. He went down to the Cape May Police station to complain, and he was agitated "to put it mildly," he added this as an aside. He raised such a stink that Diane, the Chief of Police, came out of her office confronted him and ultimately charged him with "Tumultuous Behavior." So, Ed went to court. During the trial, Ed's lawyer kept asking questions to undermine the "tumultuous behavior" rap, asking questions whose answers clearly demonstrated that even though he was outraged, Ed was very much under control. Under cross-examination, the Chief of Police was asked if she yelled or raised her voice at Mr. Sherretta at any time during the 30-second confrontation, and she reluctantly acknowledged that she did. The lawyer then wanted to know how close she came to Mr. Sherretta, and she admitted they were pretty much nose to nose in each other's face. At this point, Paul interrupted the narrative to ask if the Chief of Police was a close talker, which became the second *Seinfeld* reference of the morning, alluding to the episode featuring Elaine's new boyfriend Aaron who goes a bit overboard in entertaining Jerry's parents on one of their New York visits. Ed commented that she was more like a close screamer! During his close, Ed demanded an apology from the mayor over this whole ordeal, which he thought was his kiss of death because the judge waived the parking ticket fine, but still charged Ed the $600.00 for the "tumultuous behavior"!

As everyone was finishing up their breakfast and the dishes were bused from the table, Lisa J mentioned that later this month, she will have OLD SCHOOL appear as a backup band for her string class students to perform the song "Johnny B. Goode" at this year's spring strings concert. At a special ceremony after the show, Jim will transfer the official "count down shirts" to Lisa for her to wear over the last ten days of her stay at the Erma School of Hard Knocks.

After the check was delivered to Doug, the Calculator, for him to figure out this week's individual cost, Jim overheard someone mention *The Dick Van Dyke Show* and wanted to share few connections between *The Dick VanDyke Show* and *Seinfeld*. Before he could elaborate, Paul was quick to identify the character of Millie Helper as the woman who plays a cameo in the episode about the astronaut pen. Jim admitted that this was one of the connections and that another was the fact that the very first four or five shows in the very first season where filmed in the very same studio where *The Dick Van Dyke Show* shot its shows over its five-year run. Jim believed that some type of cosmic-comic connection was made between these two shows because of this.

As Doug disclosed that the cost for this week's festivities would be $11.00, Eddie J, who is an avid Conan viewer, mentioned that the other night, Conan had live bears appear on stage during the show. When Eddie said that Conan was just about to bring out the "masturbating bear," Paul wanted to know if the bear wore glasses, Bill Carr wanted to know if the bear had calluses, and the coup de grâce, Ed Sherretta wanted to know if the bear was declawed!

With those observations, another 'Breakfast with Dave' was adjourned on a high note until next week. Steve's Cafe 47 Diner again provided an excellent atmosphere for everyone to share in some good times and great food.

So, which one is Dave?

BREAKFAST WITH DAVE: THE TEN YEAR TOUR DIRECTORY

Aleathea's, 7 Ocean Street, Cape May, NJ. 08204

Alosi's Bistro, 5901 Ocean Ave, Wildwood, NJ 08260

Auggie's, 709 E 9th Street, Ocean City, NJ 08226

Back Bay Bistro, 1891 Bayshore Road, Villas, NJ 08251

The Bagel Time Café, 4600 Atlantic Ave, Wildwood, NJ 08260

Bella Vida Garden Café, 406 N Broadway, West Cape May, NJ 08204

Blue Plate Diner,* Bayshore Rd & Townbank Rd, N. Cape May, NJ

Blue Pig Tavern, 200 Congress Pl, Cape May, NJ 08204

The Breakfast Shop, 910 Bay Ave. Somers Point, NJ 08244

Castaway Café, 301 Bayshore Road, Villas, NJ 08251

Clary's Country Corner, 2 W Hereford Ave, CM Court House, NJ 08210

Cold Spring Grange Restaurant, 735 Seashore Rd, Cape May, NJ08204

Dino's Seaville Diner, 31 State Highway 50, Ocean View, NJ 08230

Dock Mike's, 110 Broadway, West Cape May, NJ 08204

Erma Deli, 635 Breakwater Rd, Cape May, NJ 08204

Fitzpatrick's Deli, 650 New Road, Somers Point, NJ

Flight Deck Diner, 505 Terminal Rd, Rio Grande, NJ 08242 (N.A.S.W.)

George's Place, 104 N Main St. Cape May Court House, NJ 08210

George's Place, 301 Beach Ave, Cape May, NJ 08204

The Grille, 502 Sunset Blvd, Cape May, NJ 08204

The Jelly Fish Café, 5911 New Jersey Ave, Wildwood, NJ 08260

Jimbo's Family Restaurant,* 2410 Atlantic Ave, North Wildwood, NJ

Key West Café, 4701 Pacific Ave, Wildwood, NJ 08260

Marge's Diner, 1974 N Route 9, Cape May Court House, NJ 08210

Marvis Diner, 4900 Pacific Ave, Wildwood, NJ 08260

McGlade's on the Pier, 722 Beach Ave, Cape May, NJ 08204

Mullica River Diner, 3830 Route 47, Port Elizabeth, NJ

Oceanview Restaurant, 235 Beach Ave, Cape May, NJ 08204

Pier House Restaurant, 1327 Beach Ave, Cape May, NJ 08204

Polly's Place, 9627 3rd Ave, Stone Harbor, NJ 08247

The Red Store, 500 Cape Ave, Cape May Point, NJ 08212

Rio Grande Diner, 1305 NJ-47, Rio Grande, NJ 08242

Rio Station Restaurant, 3505 U.S. 9, Rio Grande, NJ 08242

Saltwater Café, 1231 NJ-109, Cape May, NJ 08240

Star Diner & Café, 325 W Spruce Ave, North Wildwood, NJ 08260

Steve's Café 47, 189 Delsea Dr, Cape May Court House, NJ 08210

Shore Diner, 6710 Tilton Rd, Egg Harbor Township, NJ 08234

Southville Corner Diner,* 780 State Hwy. 47, South Dennis, NJ 08245

Tuckahoe Family Diner, 2050 NJ-50, Ocean View, NJ 08230

Uncle Bill's Pancake House, 3820 Bayshore Rd, N Cape May, NJ 08204

Uncle Bill's Pancake House, 4601 Pacific Ave, Wildwood, NJ 08260

Uncle Bill's Family Restaurant, 261 Beach Ave, Cape May, NJ 08204

Villas Diner, 2100 Bayshore Rd, Villas, NJ, 08251

Yianni's Café, 841 Asbury Ave, Ocean City, NJ 08226

*no longer in operation.

CPSIA information can be obtained
at www.ICGtesting.com
Printed in the USA
BVHW090842240619
551798BV00012B/373